A Grand Slam for personal development! *Win Some* is a captivating story that masterfully introduces readers to the five essential tools for nurturing fulfilling relationships. Through Sam Masterson's struggles and triumphs, we learn that true fulfillment lies in serving others and embracing a growth mindset. This book is a game-changer for anyone seeking authentic connections and personal transformation.

—JOHN C. MAXWELL, Author and Leadership Expert

I love how *Win Some* teaches us! Sam's journey takes us on a rollercoaster ride of self-awareness, reflection, and brilliant insights. Read this book and discover the power of being intentional with people, resulting in great relationships and success.

—JON GORDON, 15x Best-selling Author of
The Energy Bus and *The Carpenter*

Very few books are for everyone. This is a story we can all relate to with a message that inspires us to be better. In *Win Some*, Slipka gets real and shows the key to success and impact is in building high-trust relationships. Do you want to build a better business? Build it on trust. Learn how in this fresh, relevant, and fun story laced with inspiring truth about how to prioritize and enjoy fulfilling relationships. Every leader should read this book.

—DR. DAVID HORSAGER, CEO of Trust Edge Leadership Institute, bestselling author of *The Trust Edge*, inventor of the Enterprise Trust Index

With the steady and engrossing pace of a tightly played baseball game, Slipka unpacks the wisdom of personal transformation through the true-to-life struggles and triumphs of Sam Masterson. Masterfully written and filled with vivid imagery and captivating dialogue, *Win Some* is guaranteed to enrich your relationships in life and business. A HOME RUN!

—JOHN BUSACKER, Founder of Life-Worth and author of
Gasping for Breath and *Do Less, Be More.*

Restoring relationships. Building trust. Being vulnerable. Leading by serving. Finding purpose. An old pro's tattered life resembles a tangled mess under the torn cover of a baseball until he discovers five life-changing truths. These truths shift his focus on his scorecard of success to living a life of significance. Read, ponder, and apply the lessons learned from an unassuming, unlikely mentor.

—DR. PAUL L. H. OLSON, Executive Advisor,
Former Chairman of Entegris Inc.

Slipka's use of stories and situations resonates with a wide array of readers. For some it's a home run, but for all it helps chart a path to the bases.

—JERRY PATTENGALE, Founding Scholar, Museum of the Bible (DC),
the University Professor, Indiana Wesleyan University.

At the end of your life, what will matter to you the most? My guess is that the people you love will be toward the top of that list. At your funeral, what will people talk about? Hopefully it won't just be how much you loved a certain football team. Hopefully they will talk about how you encouraged them, served them, and cared about them. If that's what people remember, why not read a story that will help improve your relationships and develop authentic connections? That's what Brian Slipka has done in *Win Some*. It's a quick and easy read, packed with powerful principles that will change your life. Let this book guide you away from self-absorbed thinking and toward a growth mindset that puts others first. That's the life-transforming message of this book: It's not about you (or me). True fulfillment comes when we serve others. It's a powerful message that you need to read!

—**JASON STRAND**, Senior Pastor at Eagle Brook Church

Brian Slipka has consistently proven himself to be an absolute GAME CHANGER—always focused on creating unexpected momentum and building trust with others. Much like Brian, *Win Some* delivers a relatable, concise, and memorable framework for anyone with a burning desire to put some extra points on the board.

—**"TWAN" A.R. ALBANESE**, Co-Founder Duke Cannon Supply Co.®

Slipka shows a realistic and humbling example on intentionally developing the mindset of authentic and trusting relationships through Sam Masterton's story. A fulfilling read!

—**MICAH ABERSON**, President of Cambria

A personal development guide through the art of storytelling! In *Win Some*, the story of Sam Masterson's life drops pearls of wisdom masterfully woven through a rich story of struggle and triumph. No matter where you are in your life's journey, Sam's experience can provide the clarity and perspective we all seek. This book will leave you feeling inspired to live a more connected and fulfilling life.

—**MEKA WHITE MORRIS,** Executive Vice President & Chief Business Officer of the Minnesota Twins

Brian reveals the relational elements to not only be winsome, but to win in life thru deeply fulfilling relationships—RTB!

—**PJ FLECK,** Head Football Coach, University of Minnesota

WS

WIN SOME

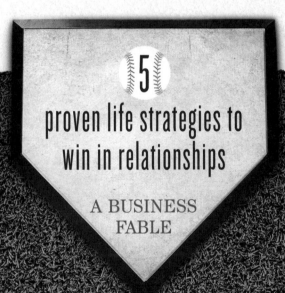

5

proven life strategies to
win in relationships

A BUSINESS
FABLE

BRIAN SLIPKA

BroadStreet
PUBLISHING

 **HORSAGER**
LEADERSHIP

BroadStreet Publishing Group, LLC.
Savage, Minnesota, USA
Broadstreetpublishing.com

Win Some
© 2024 Brian Slipka

A Horsager Leadership Press book.

9781424568642
9781424568659 eBook

Typesetting and design by Garborg Design Works | garborgdesign.com
Editorial services by Michelle Winger | literallyprecise.com

Printed in China.

24 25 26 27 28 29 30 7 6 5 4 3 2 1

DEDICATION

This book is dedicated to, first and foremost, my family: my wife, Megan, and awesome kids, Jake and Elizabeth. Words will never quite be able to express how much I love you!

I would also like to thank my True North team for putting up with me, with special thanks to Lynne, Natalie, and the holding company team.
All of you are the ultimate Winsomers!

TABLE OF CONTENTS

CHAPTER ONE

ICED CONFIDENCE

Sam Masterson gritted his teeth against a stabbing pain. He had waited until everyone headed out before taking advantage of the training room's ice bath. He hoped the freezing temperature would suck the pain from his knotted muscles. There was no need to broadcast that the team's oldest player wasn't feeling as loose and limber as his teammates.

The quiet was almost as much a relief as the numbing of his lower back and left leg. He knew the manager noticed the hitch in his stride following the play, but Sam was a master at convincing everyone around him that he was fine. No, he didn't have constant pain. No, he didn't need to see the team doctor. No, he wasn't slowing down while feeling the push to perform like a kid in his early twenties. Sam was getting good at selling the lie. He just wasn't convinced he could keep it up for much longer.

He leaned his head against the rigid rim of the tub. A persistent *drip* nearby disturbed the silence. A door slammed in the distance. The damp shower room around the corner was a breeding ground for odors. The whole place smelled of wet towels and menthol, underlaid with the ever-present odor of dirty socks.

Sam tried to think about everything except the words he'd overheard before the game. It was an effort to force his attention to his to-do list. With luck, he'd be out of the stadium within an hour. Sunset came around six thirty in Florida during March. Spring

11

training in the Sunshine State provided a welcome change to the cold, dark evenings in Minnesota at this time of year. He should make it home before sunset, but he had to pick up something for supper, make a stop at the dry cleaners for the suit a fan had spilled whiskey on at the meet-and-greet, get gas in the Explorer, and...

It was no use. Sam couldn't forget.

He had been just around the corner from the offices when he heard someone speaking across the hall. It wasn't like he meant to eavesdrop, but his name caught his attention, and he paused on the way to the locker room. He almost spoke up before he realized the men weren't talking to him, but about him.

The Minnesota club owner, Hugh Sutton, said, "Assign Masterson to train the new guy—what's his name? Anker. I want Anker to take advantage of everything he can learn from Masterson. Especially in batting. The kid is talented but needs some polish on the rough edges. I want to see some progress before we make up the season roster."

"Sure, boss. You know Masterson is going to want to know why he's on babysitting duty."

Sam knew the second voice well. He'd worked with Aaron Pinehurst for years before he left to play for the Las Vegas Springs for a couple of seasons. The man's slow drawl fooled many players into thinking they could slip something past the veteran Major League manager. Right then, Sam was more worried about what the team was up to with this new direction for his career. He came to a complete stop as they moved slowly down the hallway.

"Well, he doesn't have to know more than that the decision came straight out of the head office. Did you see the difference in his speed after that collision in the outfield today? He's getting old. I'm not saying he doesn't still have it as a hitter, but we need to get some of his experience and knowledge spread around to the guys who are going to be around for a long time."

They moved into the manager's office and closed the door without ever knowing that the subject of their conversation stood in stunned silence just around the corner.

Even the recollection of that moment reignited the sick feeling that had spread through him as he listened. Thinking about it now made him want to throw up. He'd never felt less confident in his career than he did in that moment.

There was no avoiding it. Sam was going to have to talk to someone about what his role with the Minnesota Millers club looked like going forward. If he could shed some light on the situation, he could come up with a plan to prove his continued value to the team.

The lights went out.

"Hey! Someone's still in here!" Sam yelped. Shocked out of his thoughts, he sat in freezing water in a windowless room beneath the stadium. He felt disoriented in the absolute darkness. For an instant, he had a flash of vertigo so intense he didn't know if he was still upright. He was afraid to get to his feet and attempt to step out of the tub.

> He'd never felt less confident in his career than he did in that moment.

The absence of voices and footsteps was eerie.

"Hey, turn the lights back on." He didn't know if anyone was around to hear him. "Yo! Is anyone out there?" Sam knew a raised voice in the training room could be heard in the hallway. Why wasn't the joker coming back to answer his call?

What kind of jerk didn't check to make sure the place was empty before turning off every light? Sam better not find out it was one of his teammates playing a prank. There was nothing funny about leaving a man to shiver and shrivel in an icy tub in the dark. He couldn't feel his toes anymore.

Sam debated whether he had a chance of finding his way across the floor to the nearest wall. There was a bank of switches near the towel cabinet. He hoped one of them controlled the lights in this area, otherwise he'd have to shuffle across the middle of the large room and feel his way to the door. He knew there was a light switch within a palm's reach of the doorframe.

Halfway out of the tub, Sam heard two voices echoing down the hallway. It sounded like they were coming closer.

"Hey! I'm in the training room without any light. Give me a hand, will you?"

Now footsteps slapped on the concrete floor. A few seconds later, Sam could make out the jingle of keys and realized who was in the hallway.

"Gilchrist, is that you? How about turning on some lights?"

"Hello? Is somebody in here?" The footsteps sped up as the speaker approached.

"Yes, back in the training room. Turn the lights on, man, so I can get out of this ice bath." Sam was shivering so hard his teeth clacked together when he spoke. He didn't know how long he'd been sitting in the dark, but it felt like hours.

Footsteps moved across the next room headed his way.

He heard the door to the locker room swing open a moment before the lights blazed on overhead. The sudden brightness made his eyes water.

Two figures stepped into the room, but he couldn't make them out until his eyes refocused.

"Ethan, what are you doing here? You're supposed to be in school."

"Nice to see you, too, Dad." Sam's son sneered and walked out the door.

"Wait, I didn't mean it like that." Sam surged to his feet, but his numb extremities failed him. He slipped and fell hard against the side of the tub. "Aargh!" He couldn't hold back a howl of pain as his foot slipped again, dumping him back into the icy vat. The resulting splash sent a wave of ice and water across the floor.

CHAPTER TWO

STUNNED

Sam opened his eyes as Gilchrist and Ethan pulled him above the water. His lungs burning, he choked and coughed, holding up a hand to fend them off.

"Don't," he cautioned once he could breathe. "I don't think I can get up yet."

Ethan stayed close with a hand on his dad's arm. The boy was pale, his eyes wide with anxiety. Sam hadn't seen his son so afraid since the police had come to the door to tell him that his wife had been in a serious car accident. He'd never wanted to see that look again. And now he was the cause of Ethan's distress.

"Hey, kiddo. I'll be okay in a minute." Sam cupped Ethan's chin. "Just don't go telling anyone how clumsy your dad is, okay?"

Mike Gilchrist, the Minnesota Millers' clubbie, opened a closet, grabbed a push broom, and swept water and ice toward the drain in the center of the floor. "You just stand there with your dad, Ethan, until I get this out of our way. No reason to have any more accidents tonight."

It didn't take long for him to mop up the floor. He moved back to the side of the ice bath and observed the way Sam was shivering.

"You think you can get up with our help, Sam? We need to get you warmed up and see if you hurt yourself with that fall." He reached under Sam's arm and nodded at Ethan to take his place on Sam's other side. Between the two of them, they managed to hoist

Sam high enough so he could step over the rim of the tub. They supported him for the few steps he took before collapsing on a nearby massage table.

"There are towels in that cupboard behind you, young man. Grab as many as you can, and we'll get your dad warmed up."

Ethan turned right away and filled his arms with a pile of towels. He rushed back to the table and watched as Mike wrapped Sam in several towels.

The clubbie grabbed one of Sam's feet and rubbed it briskly between his hands. "See what I'm doing here? Do you think you can do the same for your dad's arms and hands? Not too rough but strong enough to generate some warmth."

Sam watched with puzzled detachment as the boy followed the clubbie's instructions. He was amazed at the lack of argument from Ethan when Mike gave directions and expected the boy to follow them. Had Sam been the one telling him to get the towels, he'd be sitting on the table until Christmas, waiting for his son's arguments to end.

"Who are you, and what have you done with my son?" Almost before the last word left his mouth, Sam realized he'd messed up again. Ethan abruptly stopped rubbing his shoulders.

"Hmm, if you can't remember your own son, maybe you hit your head harder than we thought when you pulled your Shamu stunt." Mike walked over to a cabinet and rummaged around for the first aid kit. "Let's see if you have yourself a concussion."

Without waiting to hear what Ethan was dying to say, the clubbie handed him a small flashlight.

Ethan looked confused.

"It's never too soon to know a few life-saving tricks. Do you know how to tell if someone has a concussion?" Mike asked Ethan, ignoring the tension between father and son.

"Nope. We haven't had any Red Cross classes yet. I think we're supposed to do some things like that in PE this year."

Mike explained how to quickly shine the light into Sam's eyes and observe the reaction.

Sam noticed Ethan took some pleasure in making him squint and wince away from the bright light. But he held his breath and waited for the lesson to conclude. Until he couldn't hold back any longer.

The sound of his explosive sneeze echoed in the room. Ethan jumped back and shook his hands as if he could dislodge the germs by sheer force.

"Ewww, Dad! That's just gross. You couldn't wait until I wasn't standing right in front of you?"

He held the flashlight at the end of his extended arm unsure what to do with it.

"Sorry, sorry. I didn't know that was coming or I'd have warned you both to take cover." Sam wiped his nose on the edge of a towel.

Ethan tried to hand the flashlight to Mike who was trying not to laugh. Instead of taking the contaminated instrument, Mike gave Sam's son a disposable alcohol wipe.

"It's not funny. Dad probably just gave both of us a big booger cold." Ethan crooked his fingers, indicating he needed more wipes. Once he had a handful, he made a big production of wiping down his face, arms, and hands. "You better wipe down too, man. You don't know what kind of germs he just showered all over you." Ethan made a drama out of dropping his used wipes in the hazardous waste can in the corner of the room, leaning as far from the bin as possible while toeing the lid open.

Mike did laugh then. "Don't worry about it, young Masterson. I don't think your dad has had time to develop any serious diseases since we pulled him out of the tub. It's just a reaction to being so cold."

"If you say so." Ethan didn't look convinced, but he went about helping Mike clean up the mess they'd made of the training room. Suddenly the boy snorted. "But it was pretty funny. Did you ever hear a louder sneeze? That was like… what's the highest number on the earthquake-measuring thingy?"

"The Richter scale?"

> He seldom saw the sunny side of his boy anymore. And he didn't know what to do about that.

"Yeah, that. I bet that sneeze broke the dial. Do you think the groundskeepers felt the stadium shake?"

"While you two have a good time at the expense of my near-drowning and shriveled body parts, I'll just be in the next room getting dressed."

"Sure, go ahead, Dad. We'll be in here donning our hazmat suits."

Sam shuffled into the locker room, knowing the two were still snickering behind his back. He was glad to see his son having a good time with Mike. He seldom saw the sunny side of his boy anymore. And he didn't know what to do about that.

CHAPTER THREE

STRIKE OUT

Sam slowed to a stop at a red light ten minutes from his house. He felt especially grateful tonight for his short commute home from the new stadium.

He glanced over at Ethan, engrossed with his phone. He'd hoped the two of them could talk about something cheerful on the way home especially after the way Ethan had laughed and chatted with Mike that evening. Those two discussed the latest superhero movie all the way out of the stadium and across the parking lot to Sam's SUV. When Ethan asked Mike if they could give him a lift, the clubbie thanked him and said his car was in the lot around the corner. As Mike walked away, Ethan gazed after him.

"Come on, Son. I've got a lot to take care of tonight. Let's get on the road." Sam heard the sharpness in his tone but couldn't stop it. Why was it so easy for the boy he loved more than life to connect with a perfect stranger instead of him? It felt like one more indictment of Sam's skill in parenting since Aileen passed away. He didn't want to admit it made him more than a little jealous of the man who'd helped him that evening.

Now, as he looked at his son's face lit by the screen of his phone, Sam yearned to know how to reconnect with the little boy who used to race to the door to hug his knees every time he came home. These days he was lucky if he got a derisive grunt from Ethan—no matter when Sam came home, what he said, or what he did for the boy.

"So, you and Mike had a lot to talk about." The light turned green, and Sam eased into the intersection.

"Yeah, I guess." Ethan hardly raised his head from whatever had him enthralled on the tiny screen.

"How did you happen to be with him when you found me?"

That got his son's frowning attention. "You're kidding, right?"

"What do you mean? Why would I be kidding?" Sam felt lost already, and they'd only exchanged thirty-seven words by Sam's count. How had his innocent question sparked instant hostility yet again?

"I knew you didn't remember." Ethan threw himself back against his seat and turned his face to the window, refusing to look at his father.

"Ethan, I have no idea what you're talking about, but I'm tired." Sam put on the blinker to signal his turn into their property. "Why don't you just tell me what I've done wrong this time and get it over with? I don't have the patience for another guessing game tonight."

> "I knew you didn't remember."

Instead of answering, as soon as Sam turned off the engine, Ethan pushed his door open and stomped into the house. Sam realized Ethan had neglected to lock the door when he left for school. Again.

Sam followed slowly but reached the kitchen in time to see Ethan open the refrigerator door.

"How many times do I have to remind you to lock the back door when you leave for school, Ethan? Is it too much to ask you to pay attention to one thing?" Sam threw his keys at the bowl placed on the counter for that purpose by his late wife. "How would you feel if you came home to find someone had made off with all the nice things your mom picked out for this house?"

"Why should I care? Having her stuff around here won't bring her back!" Ethan slammed the refrigerator door hard enough to rattle the vase sitting on top.

He turned and left the room. Through the doorway, Sam saw his son throw himself on the couch in the family room, pick up the remote, and flick on the huge television screen. Moments later, the sounds of intergalactic battle bounced off the walls as Ethan increased the volume to an ear-bleeding level.

Sam strode into the room, grabbed the remote from his startled son, and savagely stabbed at the "off" button. The instant quiet was heaven to his aching head.

"Well, I care. And your mom would care. If you can't show a little respect for everything you have, then maybe you don't need anything more. That new game you wanted for your birthday? Don't be expecting it or anything else." Sam threw the remote on the chair next to the couch and crossed his arms across his chest.

"Fine. See if I care." Ethan mimicked his father's stance perfectly. "And for your information, Mom hated this house!"

Sam threw up his hands and turned his back on his son. "I don't want to hear another word from you right now. I've had all I can stand for one day. Wash your hands and get ready for supper."

"What supper? There's nothing in the refrigerator, and you didn't even stop to pick anything up."

Sam pinched the bridge of his nose. By the time he'd warmed up enough to think straight and they'd left the stadium, he'd forgotten everything on his to-do list.

He walked back into the kitchen and pulled his phone from his pocket. "What do you want on your pizza?"

"Pizza again? You know, I used to think pizza was a real treat, but after seventeen days in a row, I'm kinda over it. Order what you want. I'm not hungry." Ethan stormed out of the room.

Sam listened to the boy's sneakers slam on every tread on his way upstairs, making his irritation with his father clear. The phone in his hand started mewing like an angry cat. Ethan had reset his ringtone again. When Sam glanced to see who was calling, his headache flared.

"Dad, this isn't a good time to talk."

"Where are you? You promised you and Ethan would come by tonight."

"No, it couldn't be this evening." Sam flipped bills and unopened mail on the desk built into the kitchen counter. He finally unearthed the calendar on which he sporadically made notes about things he had to do. Once he found it, he had to flip two months forward to locate the current date. All the while, Sam's father went on and on about how he hated the rehabilitation center where he was recuperating.

"They don't even treat us like humans here. It's like being part of a herd. Where one of us goes, the rest of us must go. I'd just like to spend an afternoon in my room catching up on some reading without some lowbrow bully pushing me around. You hear me, Son? Are you even listening to what I'm saying?"

Sam snapped back, "And I'd like just one minute to myself around here without worrying about losing my job or having someone constantly blowing up over something I did or didn't do. This has been a rotten day all around. We just got home, and I'm not in the mood to turn around and drive forty minutes to listen to you complain about how hard it is at the place I'm paying for you to stay at while you recover from your back surgery. We'll get over there another day."

"But, Sam, I'm trying to tell you something important. The least you can do is listen." He could hear his dad's temper, but there was something else in the old man's voice. He didn't have the energy to figure out what it was right now. And he still had to feed his son.

"Actually, Dad," he said, "I can do less. I can hang up."

And he did.

While he had the calendar in his hand, Sam checked his notes to disprove the words Ethan had thrown at him. Seventeen days of pizza? Not possible. He was sure he'd left a note for the woman who came in to clean, asking her to make a casserole. Oh, that was a month ago.

Then he saw it. The note he'd made two weeks ago, that he'd pick Ethan up from school early today so he could show his son around the newly renovated stadium. Not only had he forgotten his promise to spend the afternoon with him, but Sam had failed to show up and check Ethan out of school.

A glance at the text messages on his phone told the rest of the story. One from Ethan's homeroom teacher about him skipping out on afternoon classes. And an earlier message from another teacher wanting to talk about grades and attitude. Sam didn't need this right now.

He dragged himself into the family room and threw himself on the couch. He snarled when his leg, back, and ribs protested. The headache he'd had since submerging in the ice bath grew fiercer as his thoughts turned angrier. Why couldn't everyone understand how hard he was working, doing all he could to take care of his family? It wasn't like anyone was helping him. Thinking about how overwhelmed he felt, Sam drifted into an uneasy doze.

CHAPTER FOUR

WHAT IS IMPORTANT

He couldn't believe he'd slept for an hour on the couch. Why hadn't Ethan woken him? Sam guessed the boy hadn't left his room and didn't even know his dad had conked out before he could organize something for supper. Forty minutes after waking with a start, Sam climbed the stairs with a loaded tray in his hands.

"Hey, I know you're mad at me. But you gotta eat, or someone will be calling Child Services on me." He listened for a response. He couldn't face the back pain he would set off if he tried to leave the tray on the floor, so he gently kicked the bottom of Ethan's bedroom door with his socked foot. "Open up." Again, no response. Finally, Sam resorted to balancing the tray on his forearm so he could free one hand to open the door.

Ethan looked up from his computer, surprised by his father's abrupt appearance in the room. Wired earpieces running to a laptop explained why he hadn't responded.

"Hey, I didn't invite you in." His indignation lasted about as long as it took to recognize the delicious aroma of grilled meat coming from the food on the tray.

"Is that an El Toro special I smell?" He quickly moved to put his laptop on the floor and pushed another pillow in place behind his back. "What's the occasion?"

"How about we call it a retreat from a constant diet of pizza?" Sam placed the tray in the middle of the comforter. "Mind if I eat with you? I'm about passing out from hunger ever since I opened the door for this delivery and smelled the steak." He tried to keep his tone casual.

Ethan hesitated a moment more than Sam hoped, then shrugged his shoulders as he reached for his favorite steak fajita dish and started piling on extra guacamole. "Well, you did get all the stuff I like, so I guess I'll let it slide this time. And you went all fancy with real plates and silverware and everything."

Relieved by more than his son's attitude, Sam took a seat on the end of the bed and reached for the plate of pollo loco. "Don't get the idea this can become a habit. It's still 'no dishes in the bedroom, only paper plates.' This is a one-time deal."

"Whatever." Ethan spoke around a mouthful, "So why tonight?"

Sam sighed and stretched his legs in front of him. "Let's mark it down as an apology for not keeping track of what I've been feeding you." He ate in silence for a minute. "I'm really sorry I forgot about our plans for this afternoon. I had a lot on my mind and then—well, it really doesn't matter why. I didn't keep my promise."

Staring at his plate, Ethan mumbled, "I kinda figured something else came up. It usually does, so I wasn't too surprised. Anyway, I just called an Uber and went out to the stadium. I thought we were going to stop and visit Grandpop on the way home."

"Yeah, another person I let down today. I've been making a habit of that lately." This time Sam couldn't keep a bite of bitterness from his voice, and he watched Ethan pull into himself. "Hey, it's not on you, buddy. You're the kid, and I'm the father. It's up to me to get things done. But we are going to have a conversation about those messages from your school about ditching. And what's this I hear about falling grades and giving your teacher attitude?"

Even as he said the words, Sam wondered why they made him feel so sick and inadequate. He was trying to take care of his family exactly the way his father taught him when he was Ethan's age. Every time he turned around, he'd offended someone new or done the wrong thing. Why did life work for everyone else but him?

He watched his son roll his eyes and turn a shoulder.

Sam's appetite disappeared. He put his half-eaten dinner back on the tray and stood. "Guess I'll get out of here and let you get to sleep. It's a school day tomorrow, and we'll have to leave early so I can check you in after your unexplained absence. Finish your supper and make sure you get that plate down to the kitchen no later than tomorrow morning. I don't want to walk in here one day and find a science experiment under your bed." He didn't mean it to sound like an accusation, but he could see Ethan took it that way.

"Sure. Whatever." Ethan had already tuned him out, hunching over his plate in frustration.

Outside the door he'd just pulled shut, Sam stood lost in the raw grief that struck him at unexpected moments. He'd lost the love of his life even before the actual accident that took her away from their little family. Now he felt he was losing their son. And he had absolutely no idea how to stop it.

* * *

After locking up the house, Sam lay in bed, arms crossed beneath his head, and stared at the ceiling.

He still slept on "his" side, never choosing to move to the middle of the bed even though there was no reason not to take all the space. Every morning as soon as he woke, and every night before he fell asleep, he ran his hand across the empty side of the bed and smoothed the unused pillow.

Sam missed his wife with an ache made worse by the fact that they'd been growing apart the last year of their time together. Aileen had wanted him to spend more time with the family, to be more present when he was there. And Sam had wanted to make her proud, to protect her the way his father had taught him by making enough money so she and Ethan never had to go without anything they needed or wanted. He repeatedly tried to explain why he had taken the job in Las Vegas playing for their Major League team, the Springs, for a few seasons. The money, he told her, was too good to pass up. He could hear her reply even now in his mind.

"Don't you know what's important anymore?"

"Sam, these are the best years of our life as parents, and you are missing them for money! Ethan is a teenager and he needs you. I need you too. Don't you know what's important anymore?" The memory brought sudden tears to his eyes.

Sam knuckled his eyes dry. Crying never solved anything. His father had told him this the day his mother passed away. *Just get on with doing what needs to be done.*

He reached over and turned the lamp off. Facing the emptiness across the bed, he reached out and fell asleep with his hand resting on his wife's pillow.

CHAPTER FIVE

A BIG ERROR

By Saturday, Sam had no choice but to make a trip to the grocery store. He invited Ethan along, thinking they could make it family time. But he'd been unprepared for the pushy crowds snatching up food ahead of Spring Break, which would start the following Monday. The store was a madhouse.

Sam disliked shopping. He and Ethan had gotten into the habit of throwing a ready-to-eat dinner into the microwave whenever they got hungry. He knew his son's newfound opinion about ordering pizza every night. Sam was glad he'd convinced Ethan to join him. If he allowed the boy to choose what he wanted to eat next week, there shouldn't be a lot of room for complaints. On the other hand, nothing had made much difference in his son's attitude lately.

Ethan yanked a cart out of the corral and leaned on the handle as if he were so tired that he couldn't support himself. When Sam headed toward the fresh produce section, Ethan dragged his feet but followed.

"Why didn't we shop yesterday when it wasn't so busy?"

"Because you had to stay after school, and I had to meet with your teachers because you skipped on Thursday."

"So? We still could have stopped on the way home. Then we wouldn't have to be dodging all these idiot breakers." Ethan watched a local woman face off with three frenzied college kids over possession of the last bag of rippled chips.

"Hey! You don't call anyone names. You know that. What's gotten into you?" Sam dropped a bag of apples into the cart.

"Whatever." Ethan threw up his hands and walked away.

"If you're so worried about it, get back here and help me with this list so we can get out of here faster." Sam didn't raise his voice, but he knew Ethan heard him. His son wasn't the only one who didn't like to shop when the store was busy. Why couldn't they suffer equally?

After tossing a couple tomatoes and heads of lettuce into the cart, Sam took off in pursuit of his son. The boy was getting harder to handle every day.

When he caught up to Ethan, Sam tore the list in half and handed him one piece. "Get only what's on the list. Meet me by the cereal aisle."

"Why do I have to get all the canned stuff? They are too hard to carry without the cart." Ethan glared at the torn paper in his hand.

> The boy was getting harder to handle every day.

"Fine." Sam grabbed the list from Ethan and thrust the other half into his son's hand. "If it will get us out of here faster, I'll do the canned goods. Now stop making this harder than it is. Just do what I ask for once." This time it was a challenge to control the level of his voice. He looked around to see if anyone was listening to their argument.

"Don't worry. We can't get out of here fast enough to suit me. This sucks."

Sam opened his mouth, but before he could discipline Ethan for his backtalk, the boy was at the end of the aisle and gone from sight. He closed his eyes and rubbed the bridge of his nose. Hard. Why couldn't he have a kid who listened and obeyed without question?

By the time Sam finished his half of the list, Ethan was waiting in the cereal aisle, tapping his foot. As soon as Sam stopped next to him, Ethan dumped bread, boxes of spaghetti, mac and cheese, and finally, a case of sports drinks on top of the contents.

Biting his tongue, Sam rearranged the items in the cart to prevent the heavier stuff from smashing the fruit, vegetables, and bread. After one more look at his half of the list, he turned the cart around and headed for the checkout stations.

The self-check lines were several people deep, so he wheeled into an open station and unloaded his cart onto the conveyor belt. The middle-aged clerk greeted him with the standard, "Did you find everything you were looking for today?" It was only then that she looked up.

Sam saw the moment she identified him. She caught her breath, nearly choking with excitement.

"Oh my, oh my goodness! I can't believe I get to check out Slammin' Sammy! Can I just tell you how excited I am that you're back with the Millers this year? Why, I sure never expected to see someone famous shopping here. Wait 'til I tell all my friends. Could I just get a selfie with you?"

Without waiting for an answer, the frizzy-haired clerk pulled a phone from her pocket, turned her back to him, and held it at arm's length to take the shot. She inspected the result and pouted.

"Oh, wait. You weren't smiling. Let me get another one." She ignored Sam's frowning dissent and snapped a second photo.

Behind him, Sam heard a snort of derision and a not-so-quiet "Jeez, can't we go anywhere without running into all your fans?" He deliberately stepped on Ethan's toe and elbowed him in the ribs, hoping he'd take the hint to stop talking.

"Look"—Sam read the name on her employee badge—"Darla, I'd prefer you delete those photos. I'm just trying to grab some groceries and get out of here." He glanced over his shoulder to find the line of shoppers behind him was steadily growing impatient with the delay at the counter. "Will you please delete those photos? This is my private life."

Darla grudgingly pressed a few keys on the phone and shoved it back into her pocket. Sam could only hope she'd done as he asked.

All hope of getting quickly through the line died when Ethan moved out from behind his father. Darla's hands went to her mouth while she let out a high-pitched squeal. Anyone who hadn't been paying attention to her checkout line was now straining to see what was happening.

"Oh, this must be your son. He looks just like you." She turned to Ethan and demanded, "I bet you're just as good at baseball as Slammin' Sammy, aren't you, sweetie? You must be so proud of your father. How exciting to have a dad who's the best hitter in the league!"

Ethan scowled furiously before hunching his shoulders and staring at the floor. Sam could see his son shrinking into himself. What did they have to do to get out of this store?

"Aw, what a cutie. He's shy." The clerk giggled and made a little waving motion at Ethan with her fingers, oblivious to the boy's distress.

"Darla, we're really in a hurry. Can you get us checked out here?" He was holding onto his temper, but he could hear the buzz of excitement around him as more shoppers realized who he was.

"Well, sure, Sammy. I hope you don't mind me calling you that. It's just that I've always been one of your biggest fans. Why I remember when—"

"I appreciate that, Darla, I really do. Thank you for following my career. But my son and I are tired and hungry. We want to get home."

"Right, right," Darla scanned a few more items and shoved them in the bagger's direction. Sam stopped her when she ran a case of super-caffeinated energy drinks across the electronic eye.

"Wait. That isn't mine." He looked at the counter and saw several things from his cart still on the belt. "I didn't pick that up."

Before Darla could reverse the sale on the case, Ethan spoke up. "It's mine. I put it on the counter."

"We've talked about this, Ethan. I'm not bringing that stuff into the house. You know the rules."

"Well, Mom's not here to enforce them now, is she? It's a stupid rule, anyway. All the kids at school drink this every day, and it hasn't hurt any of them." Ethan's voice rose as his face turned red with temper.

"You're not those other kids. And don't bring your mother into this. I'm telling you no." Sam couldn't believe Ethan was pulling this stunt in public. "We are not having this discussion now. And especially not here."

"Oh, come on, Sammy. He wants to be like the other kids. There's nothing wrong with that. Hey, I drink this stuff, and I'm just..." Darla fell silent when Sam turned to face her.

"I don't need you or anyone else to tell me how to raise my son. The only thing I require from you is to get my groceries checked out so I can get the hell out of here. And I would prefer you to do that in silence. Do you think you can manage that, Darla? Or should I ask the manager to find someone who can?"

The bagger at the end of the counter dropped three cans of green beans. They rolled across the floor, loud in the sudden silence at the front of the store.

A chorus of gasps and muffled words broke the hush surrounding the drama. Sam felt the shocked reactions from shoppers in his line and the ones on either side. Then the whispers started. He heard his name along with comments about rude, entitled athletes. When he turned his head, he faced a couple dozen cell phones recording the scene.

Ethan pushed past him and raced out of the store. That caught the attention of even more shoppers, who quickly focused on the line where the red-faced clerk was slamming the last few items through the scanner. The bagger retrieved the canned vegetables but was shaking so hard he could barely finish sacking the groceries.

Sam closed his eyes for an instant in disgust. There was no way he could convince the onlookers to delete those photos. And videos. Everyone took videos of everything these days.

He opened his wallet and tapped his card at the terminal to pay for his order.

The bagger looked scared when he opened his mouth. "Do y-you need help getting your b-bags to—"

"I've got it. Thanks." Sam took the cart the boy pushed in his direction and strode from the store.

Way to go, Sam, he thought. *You just blew up in front of a few dozen people who have probably sent photos and videos to all their friends. And to top it off, the father and son bonding-over-groceries-idea became one more opportunity to make your son hate you.*

CHAPTER SIX

CAUGHT LOOKING

Sam's eyes were still half-shut when he strolled into the kitchen in his pajamas the following morning. Ethan hunched over a bowl of cereal, arms wrapped around it as if it were about to escape. He didn't acknowledge his father's presence, so Sam knew the boy was punishing him for the embarrassment and refusal to buy those drinks.

He didn't have the energy to comment on the amount of milk Ethan had used to drown his breakfast or that the milk jug sat open on the table. Sam picked up the gallon jug he'd bought yesterday, observed that it was down two-thirds, and screwed the lid back on.

"How about some pancakes to go with that? I'll even fry up some eggs if you're hungry enough." Sam opened the refrigerator to return the milk to its shelf. While in there he pulled out the egg carton, some cheese, and a package of bacon. "What do you say, Ethan?"

When he turned back to his son, the boy shook his head. "Nah."

"Nah, what?"

Ethan smirked. "Nah, thanks."

"Did you bring the paper in yet?" Sam cracked a couple of eggs in a small skillet and stirred them with a spatula. He laid three strips of bacon in another pan before he looked at his son.

Ethan shrugged. "I guess the delivery kid is late today." The way he ducked his head and avoided his father's eyes looked suspicious.

34

Sam was about to question his son further when the doorbell rang. They both turned to look at the clock on the stove.

"Who shows up at 7:15 on a Sunday morning? Did you invite one of your buddies over?" The visitor was leaning on the doorbell now. "Keep your eye on those pans, will you? I don't want to get back here and find my breakfast burned to cinders."

Ethan groaned but got up from his chair to take the spatula from his father's hand. "You're the one with the reputation for setting the kitchen on fire, Dad."

The doorbell pealed over and over.

"Hey, Dad…" Ethan stopped Sam as he reached the doorway to the kitchen. The doorbell sounded eight times in quick succession. "Never mind. Better see who that is."

Sam hesitated another few seconds. There was definitely something going on, but he didn't have time for it. Right now, he had to go yank that doorbell off the wall.

* * *

Geoff Mark jerked his finger off the button when Sam threw open the door. He looked as startled to see Sam as Sam was to see him.

"Geoff. What are you doing here and why are you in such a hurry?" Sam held out his hand to his agent who ignored the gesture. He pushed past Sam and shoved the door almost closed. The man who had negotiated Sam's contracts since he started with the majors peered around the door as if he expected a storm of sharks to fall into the front yard at any moment.

Geoff shoved the door closed and turned the lock. Only then did he face Sam.

"Why aren't you answering your phone or my texts? Do have any idea what's going on?"

Sam led the way back to the kitchen. Ethan nodded to Geoff and handed Sam a plate onto which he'd scraped the overdone eggs and underdone bacon.

"Hey, Mr. Mark. I'll be in my room." Ethan was out of the kitchen and halfway up the stairs before Sam could say a word.

"Sam, I've been calling your cell, your landline, and texting every five minutes since six this morning. You can't just blow this off. You can't just blow me off. It's my job to represent you, but so help me, you've made it nearly impossible."

"Wait, you said you've been calling since six this morning? How could I not hear the phone ring for an hour and fifteen minutes?" Sam strode to the den and picked up the landline phone, following the cord back to the wall. He held up the unplugged end and eyed his agent.

"Well, that explains why no one could reach you on that antique." Geoff didn't seem much happier. "What about your cell?"

"It's on my bedside table." Sam went to plug in the landline, but Geoff took it out of his hands.

"Leave it for now. I'll go get your cell. You put on a pot of coffee. You're going to want to be awake for this." He headed for the stairs and called back, "Make my coffee Irish. Very, very Irish."

When Sam walked into the kitchen, he saw a crumpled newspaper sticking out of the trash can next to the French doors to the lanai. He pulled it out and pressed the wrinkles out of it. It was that day's edition.

Sam felt sick. The only way the newspaper could have ended up in the trash was if Ethan put it there.

Geoff swept back into the kitchen with Sam's cell and tablet. He dumped them on the table before grabbing the paper from Sam's hands. "Where's the coffee? Do I have to do everything myself?"

"You might as well tell me what's going on. It's evident Ethan unplugged the landline and threw away today's paper. I suppose my cell somehow mysteriously turned itself off in the middle of the night?"

"Looks that way, mate." Geoff couldn't have a conversation without throwing in at least one nautical term. Sam usually found it amusing. Today it rubbed his nerves raw.

"Look," Geoff had the coffee machine filled and turned on. "I'm not saying it's your fault, but things could be better." He rummaged in one of the upper cabinets until he found the Irish whiskey

Sam pulled out only for parties. "And I'm not ready to talk about it without some fortification."

Since his agent refused to talk, Sam grabbed the newspaper and spread it open to the first page. He thought he would throw up when he saw the headline.

"Slammin' Sam Loses It at the Grocery Store."

The story beneath the two-inch banner was just as sensational. And there were photos. Someone had managed to get a shot that caught Sam leaning toward the woman while she looked at him with sheer resentment. In the background, Ethan's face reflected anger and embarrassment.

Sam dropped the paper onto the table and groaned. "I'm guessing everyone's seen this story by now. It's not what it looks like."

"Yeah, I've never heard that line from a client before." Geoff placed a mug of coffee in front of Sam. "And it's not only the *News Journal*. There are stories just like this or worse on every television news channel, including the cable guys. And then there are the videos on YouTube and Twitter. I have to say, you seldom mess up, Masterson. But when you do, you make up for lost time."

"What do I do now? Should I go back to the store and apologize to the clerk?" Sam felt horrible about how he'd treated the woman. He hadn't realized how menacing he'd looked, not to mention how he must have sounded, until seeing the front-page photo.

Geoff shook his finger at Sam. "You don't go near that woman. You don't say anything to reporters. Don't try to explain or apologize. You just lay low. I'll see what I can do to clean this up."

"Yeah, and how will you do that?" Sam didn't agree. His mother would have been ashamed to hear how he spoke to someone who was simply excited to meet him. And she would have been right. But his agent was telling him to act as if nothing had happened. And that didn't sit right with Sam's conscience.

"I'm warning you, Sam. If you get out there and start talking about what you really meant, or why you were angry, or how your blood sugar was low, and you couldn't help yourself… well that'll only encourage more talk and more people sharing those photos and videos."

Sam shook his head. "It doesn't feel right to just ignore this."

"Sam, my man, how long have I been your agent?" Geoff leaned back and crossed his arms.

"I guess it's sixteen years this year. Why?"

"Have I ever steered you wrong in all that time?" Now his agent looked smug.

"I guess not." But looking back, Sam couldn't help thinking that Geoff's advice about moving to Las Vegas temporarily hadn't been all that great. That decision had been the beginning of his marital problems.

"Then you can trust me now. I'm not going to let you end up like those athletes who stand in front of the world and try to talk their way out of bad behavior. I'm here to tell you that it never works. Just keep your mouth shut and focus on baseball. That's my advice."

> "Just keep your mouth shut and focus on baseball."

Geoff stood up and moved his empty mug and Sam's untouched coffee to the side. "The first thing we must do is make a strategy to turn the conversation to something or someone else. And I'm not leaving here today until we've got a plan." He grabbed his briefcase from under the table and pulled out a legal pad.

"No," Sam said.

"What do you mean, 'no'? If you think today's news is bad, wait until you see what it looks like twenty-four hours from now." Geoff was as grim as Sam had ever seen him.

Sam stood up and shoved his chair into place under the table. "No, as in, I'm going to go upstairs and talk to my son. If you intend to wait until we come back down, make yourself useful and load the dishwasher."

Geoff stared after him as Sam walked out of the room.

As he walked up the stairs, he wondered what he could say to apologize to Ethan.

CHAPTER SEVEN

ON PROBATION

The next day, Sam arrived at the training facility before 7:00 a.m. When he'd turned his cell on the previous day, it chimed like crazy while delivering a backlog of voice messages and texts. He'd quit counting after eighty-nine voice messages and two hundred and ten texts. The one that caught his attention was from Hugh Sutton. The new Millers owner did not mince words.

"Masterson, my office Monday morning, 7:30."

Sam suspected he was about to find out whether he still had a job.

Five minutes later, Sam knocked on the door labeled "The Boss Man Lives Here."

"Come in."

When Sam stepped inside the office, Sutton didn't look up, giving Sam time to look beyond the massive mahogany desk, through the floor-to-ceiling windows, right out onto the stadium field. The grass was a richer, deeper green from this elevation. At this hour, only a handful of staff moved around the dugout and worked maintenance tasks around the infield.

"Good morning, sir."

Sutton took his time before raising his gaze from the contents of a folder on the otherwise empty desk. "Oh, it's you."

Sam hadn't spent much one-on-one time with the new team owner, but the man didn't sound happy to see him.

"Sit down, and let's get this over with. I've got a million things on my schedule today."

Sam's boss folded his hands over the papers and leaned forward as if to impart some intimate news.

"I cannot tell you how extremely disappointed I was to wake up yesterday and read a series of appalling headlines about one of my players. And then I saw the videos. Do you have any idea how many phone calls I received from friends and reporters? Important people wanting to know why one of my players was yelling at a store clerk? Did you go out of your way to make me look bad, Masterson? Or does that come naturally to you?"

"No, sir. I apologize. It's been a rough week—"

His boss slashed through Sam's contrition. "It's too late for an apology, boy."

Bubbling through his mortification, Sam felt a spark of resentment at the demeaning *boy*. Sutton was at least ten years younger than Sam. The shorter man apparently used his authority to feel like a bigger man. And he wasn't done yet.

"I don't care how rough your life is. I don't care if your kitten ran away, a hurricane leveled your mother's house, or a gator ate your dog. If you ever do anything to make me look bad again, you're finished."

Sam could only breathe through his nose. His jaw was so tight he doubted he'd be able to speak if he could get a word in edgewise.

Sutton shook a finger in Sam's face.

"The former owner may have been your good buddy and brought you back here after you flamed out in Las Vegas, but you're next to nothing in my book. You're only here because Earl Knight had a soft spot for you. He must have been senile when he signed the deal to bring you back here. When I bought out Knight, the Springs told me if I wanted Anker, I had to honor your contract first. I was stuck with you then, but I don't have to keep you."

That was a real blow to any ego he had left. Sam thought his day couldn't get worse. He could barely see straight.

"You'd better cool down right now, Masterson. After yesterday, you don't have a leg to stand on if I tell everyone you have a problem with your temper. Give me an excuse."

There was no way to answer that corny threat. So, Sam stared at the bridge of Sutton's nose, enduring the seconds until he could leave the guy's office. And to think he'd been so excited to rejoin his old team. If only he'd known before his contract went through that Earl Knight had plans to sell the Millers.

Sutton pulled the papers together, tapped them on the desk to even the edges, and placed them in the folder. He made a couple minute adjustments to its placement before sitting back in his chair.

Sam felt every year of his age as he stood up to leave.

"Here's all you need to know, Masterson. It's my name on your checks. I'm giving you one chance to make this work. One screwup, and we will release you. I don't care what your contract says. My lawyers are bigger and meaner than yours, and they'll take pleasure in terminating you for violating the morals clause. You remember signing that, don't you?

"You're going to play your little heart out for me in every game. And you're going to show Anker everything you know about hitting. If you can do that without me hearing any talk about your attitude or behavior, you might keep playing here next year."

The Boss Man stared at Sam, daring him to speak. Then he turned his chair to face the window. "You're dismissed."

Sam felt every year of his age as he stood up to leave. He was back in the hallway less than five minutes after entering the office. He was mentally exhausted, but he needed to change and get out on the practice field. Sutton was salivating for a reason to fire him. Sam thought he must be hearing things when the theme of *The Good, The Bad, and the Ugly* filtered through the closed office door.

CHAPTER EIGHT

PILING ON

If he'd ever had any doubt about how far the news had spread, it ended as soon as he walked into the locker room. A clamor of laughing and shouting died once his teammates realized Sam had arrived.

"Oh, Jonesy, I'm such a fan." Keenan Quinn pitched his voice into a squeak and fluttered his eyelashes at teammate D'Andre Jones. Keenan tossed his head, though it didn't stir his crew cut out of place. "Do say you'll let me take a selfie! I promise to gaze adoringly at it for the rest of my life."

Jones struck a pose with both hands on his hips, nose tilted into the air. "The only thing I require from you is that you get your fat behind off my towel."

The locker room erupted with catcalls and laughter, each player trying to outdo the next with rude remarks.

After his session with Sutton, Sam didn't have the heart to joke around with the guys. He couldn't even pretend their jokes didn't matter. It took every ounce of his energy to change into his practice uniform. He knew he'd pay for not responding.

Sure enough, when his teammates exited the locker room, several shoved past him on their way out. They made no attempt at subtlety with their comments about prima donnas with bad tempers.

Sam was tying his cleats when the door slammed open again. Club Manager Aaron Pinehurst, and another man strode into the room.

"Sam, glad we caught you."

"Hey, Aaron. What's up?" Busy with closing his locker, Sam didn't pay much attention to the young man with Pinehurst.

"This here's Jakob Anker. The boss man says he's your new protégé. Jakob, meet Slammin' Sam Masterson. He's just come back to us from out West, where he played for the Las Vegas Springs for a couple seasons. Hey, didn't you guys come from the same team?" Aaron looked from one man to the other. "You probably knew each other there?"

"It's an honor to meet you, Mr. Masterson, sir." Jakob stuck out his hand.

Sam met the nervous young player's eyes. "I think I was leaving Vegas the week you came up from the minors. I heard your name around the club but don't remember working with you."

Jakob nodded his head. "Yeah, I got lucky. Mr. Sutton saw me at a charity game and decided he wanted me on the team he'd just bought. The Springs manager said he refused to take no for an answer, so they let me go along with some older guy."

Aaron groaned and gave Sam the side-eye to see his reaction.

"Yeah, I heard. Seems the guys who make those decisions see your potential as a hitter. So, I guess it's time for this old guy to see what you've got." Sam snickered as he headed for the door, not waiting to see if anyone followed.

Jakob's eyes widened as he looked at Aaron who shrugged and nodded.

"Well, hell. Way to make friends on your first day," Jakob muttered, then took off to catch up with Sam.

* * *

Sam was the only player still in the locker room when Mike Gilchrist wandered in at the end of the day. The clubbie stopped short when he saw Sam sitting in front of his locker, elbows on his knees with his hands clamped atop his head.

"Sorry, Sam. I didn't know anyone was still here. Didn't mean to disturb you." Mike turned to leave.

"Hey, wait. You're not disturbing anything I wouldn't rather forget." Sam beckoned the man back. "I'm in your way. Won't be the first time today. I'll be out of here in a few minutes." Sam stood up and started stuffing workout clothes and towels into his duffel.

"Rough day?" Mike raised one foot to the bench and leaned his forearms on his knee.

Sam blew a huff of bitter amusement. "Rough day. Rough week. Rough everything. Feels like it just keeps piling on, and I don't even know where to find a shovel."

Taking a seat on the bench, Mike motioned for Sam to stop and join him.

"Is this about the grocery store incident?"

"Oh, boy, Mike. If only that were all. I feel like I'm drowning, but I can't even do that right. I'm the one who's supposed to be saving my kid, and my dad, and this new guy. I'm the last person anyone should look to for help, but it's my job to be there. Except I'm not, really. And every time I open my mouth, I stick my entire leg into it. I made the new guy self-conscious before practice even got started today. Then it sounded like everything I suggested was a criticism." Sam stood up and hefted his duffel onto his good shoulder. "Sorry, man! Bet you didn't expect a pity party when you walked in here. I didn't mean to dump on you, Mike. I'm just going to get out of here and let you get on with whatever."

> "I'm the last person anyone should look to for help, but it's my job to be there."

Sam slammed his locker and spun the lock. He didn't want to look the clubbie in the eye, fearing he'd see disgust or pity for his outburst.

"I thought your job with Jakob Anker was to make him a better batter."

"Yeah. That's the idea. But I can't do that without telling the guy what he's doing wrong. Then he gets shook up and his swings get worse. If I can't make him look better, he won't get a batting position, and Sutton will kick my butt out of here."

Mike took his time standing and stretching like he had no better place to be. "I don't know about you, but I could sure do with a good cup of coffee right about now. How about you let me buy you a cup, and I'll tell you why you've got to be winsome?"

CHAPTER NINE

GRAB YOUR BAT

"Wait Mike, I must have misheard you. What does being childlike and charming have to do with me keeping my job or mending fences with my family? To be honest, I'm not quite sure how that looks on a six-foot, 209-pound frame. Are you setting me up to compete for the Miss Congeniality sash?" Sam stopped and pulled out a chair at a small table in the corner of the coffee shop.

He and Mike sat down at the same time, but Sam could tell Mike was the far more relaxed of the two.

"No, I don't want you to compete for anything, Sam. You don't have to win anything to win everything." Mike leaned back and sipped his coffee.

> "You don't have to win anything to win everything."

"You've totally lost me, buddy. What are you talking about?" Sam raised his cup and blew some heat off it while waiting for Mike to make sense.

"It's just a matter of where you place your emphasis. I'm not talking about winsome, like the Girl Scout selling cookies outside the pharmacy. Although there's no rule that baseball players can't wear a congeniality sash if they want."

Sam snorted.

Mike grabbed a napkin, pulled a pen from his pocket, and wrote the letters. Then he turned the flimsy paper to face Sam.

Win Some.

Mike gestured toward the words. "See what I mean about placing the emphasis? Well, being Win Some is all about how you place emphasis on things in your life. And when you get it right, you don't win everything in your life, but you win the important things. And so does everyone around you."

"What do you mean by 'winning the important things'? I'm paid to win. That's my job." Sam drummed his fingers on the table, hoping he hadn't wasted his time by agreeing to meet Mike.

"Nope. You're paid to help your team win. And you have a skewed perspective on what winning means when you think it's all on you." Mike was matter-of-fact about calling Sam out.

"So, what's your definition of winning?" The sarcasm came through, though Sam tried to temper it.

Mike leaned forward as if to impart a secret.

"When you win, someone else has to lose."

"Well, yeah. That's how it works. Our team wins, the other team loses. We get a bonus, and our team goes home happy."

"If you want to measure winning by the size of your bonus, have I got some good news for you. Let me buy this round, and I'll tell you why your life starts to improve today."

> "When you get it right, you don't win everything in your life, but you win the important things."

Sam shook his head in disbelief but waved an okay over his empty cup. "Just promise me I'm not signing up to hear an hour-long sales pitch for some multi-level marketing scheme."

Heads turned in the coffee shop when Mike unleashed a belly laugh. "You've got my word on that, Sam."

With fresh coffee in front of them, Sam asked the question foremost in his mind. "You don't really know me that well, Mike. I mean, we talk when we run into each other at the stadium, but we've never spent that much time together. What makes you so sure you can help me turn my life around without knowing what's going on?"

"Because this framework works for anyone who knows it and applies it."

"Before we go any further, Mike, I gotta ask. Are you trying to get me to join a church? I've seen that cross you wear around your neck. I'm not into religion at all. I know some of the guys on the team pray before games, and that's fine for them, but you are never going to get me into a pew on Sunday mornings. I had enough of that when I was growing up. Church is not for me."

Mike leaned back in his chair and looked straight at Sam for a long moment before he answered. "No. I'm not recruiting you for Sunday services. I'm not going to lie, my faith is very important to me, but I don't have any agenda except to help you. Win Some is not about religion at all. It's more like a philosophy."

Sam couldn't stop the snort of derision escaping. He crossed his arms across his chest, leaned back in his chair, and said, "That sounds pretty fishy to me."

Mike smiled, "I've known you a long time, and it's easy to see that you are in a bad place right now. I know the signs; I've been there too. In fact, my dark days cost me a lot. However, I got lucky, and someone helped me out of that hole by teaching me how to be Win Some before I lost everything. I thought you might trust me enough to listen to some ideas."

"Well, don't keep me waiting. Explain this thing you're so excited about." Sam sat back, prepared to hear a bunch of woo-woo stuff, although he hadn't pegged Mike as someone who went for that.

"First, I want you to think about how you approach the game on the field. You and the team are united in purpose. And everything you do that day prepares you to help make that happen."

"So? Did you drag me here to give me a lesson in how to play ball?"

"Not at all. That's one thing you know how to do, and you do it well."

"Gee thanks. I was hoping that I could do several things well." Though he knew Mike probably hadn't meant it that way, Sam felt more than a twinge of worry that this was exactly what Mike was telling him.

"Come on, you know me better than that. I'm saying you are a very disciplined and diligent athlete. You can use that discipline to control your mind so you can influence and connect with the people around you."

"I'm not making the connection."

"It's simple. Do you trust me?"

"Sure, you've always been strai   with me."

"Trust develops over time   can't be Win Some until you build trust. There's a drama   rence between how you approach baseball and how   t with people. And they're at oppo-site ends of th   n. Your teammates trust you to be in the game wi   ou all stand together, like a brotherhood, shoul-der-t   der. I see you working with your teammates as a team. Y   al is to help the team do the best it can that day."

"Okay. What's your point about me interacting with people?" nce that seemed to be his most prevalent misstep these days, Sam was at least willing to listen even if Mike blasted him for the way he'd behaved at the store.

"That's where I see a totally different side of you. You make it all about you. It's like watching one of those old Westerns where the gunslingers face off with each other in the middle of the street at high noon. It's your way or the highway, a win-lose situation."

"Wow. That's harsh. But since I obviously don't know how to talk with my own kid without starting a minor war, it's probably true." Sam took a deep breath and forced his fingers through his unruly brown hair. "That's not my intention, ever, but now that I hear how you describe it, I can see how it might look that way to everyone. I still don't get what this Win Some idea is about."

Mike paused to think, then asked, "Are you satisfied with your relationship with Ethan? What about your relationships with the team? Are they fulfilling to you?"

"Satisfied? Fulfilling? What are you talking about? I'm just trying to get through my day. I don't think about stuff like that," Sam snorted.

"Well, maybe you should give it some thought. From what I see, you don't seem very happy. In fact, you look pretty frustrated most of the time."

"Oh… well, if you want me to be blunt, things are not going too great for me right now." Sam looked at the floor and crossed his arms across his chest.

"So, if you are not happy with your relationships, it seems like a perfect time to try something else. Right?"

After Sam's begrudging nod, Mike continued, "Being Win Some means that you are comfortable enough with yourself that you can come alongside others and help them, without selfish ambition. If you can let other people *win*"—Mike made quote marks with his fingers—"some of the things they want or need, that means you win some of the things you want too."

"Are you trying to snow me? How can we both win?"

"By making a choice before you talk with someone. Would you rather be the person who wins every argument and loses his family, friends, and potentially his job, or the person who helps others? That's the person who creates positive relationships and finds even more fulfillment than focusing on themselves!"

"That's not a hard choice. Anyone would want to be the second guy. But what if you don't know how? I was taught to win regardless of the cost." Sam's throat ached as he posed the question to the clubbie.

"You don't have to keep doing something that's not working. You just decide to aim for win-win interactions instead of win-lose. That's how you build trust with the people around you."

"I don't know about that trust thing, Mike. Seems like my teammates hate me for going to Las Vegas and hate me more for coming back." Pushing his cup away, Sam stuffed his hands into the pockets of his jacket and slumped in his chair. "Some of them haven't spoken to me since I returned."

Mike tapped the table in front of Sam to get his attention. "That's what I'm talking about. Have you made the effort to connect with the guys who haven't talked to you? Some of them probably feel like they don't know you any longer. Las Vegas is a long way, in more than one way, from Minnesota. They may be afraid you'll think they're just hicks. After all, you've been to big old Sin City, and they stayed here."

Sam felt shocked by Mike's perspective. "Now I feel even worse. You mean all I had to do was say hi, and there wouldn't be all this awkwardness? I'm over here feeling like the new guy, and they're over there feeling like they don't know me anymore? What a mess."

"It's not as bad as you're thinking. And I'm sure some of the guys have never had a death in their family, so part of it is that they don't know what to say to a man who lost his wife so recently."

Mike watched over the rim of his coffee cup while the ball player processed what he was hearing. Finally, Sam leaned back and stretched his legs out.

"I don't even know what to do with what you're saying. Of course I want to be the guy who does the win-win deal. But I have no idea how to start. You sound like you have it all sewn up. Where do I go from here?"

Both men leaned toward each other across the table, one anxious to learn, the other happy to help.

"Remember when I said you have to think about how you play ball?"

Sam nodded.

"So, when you grab your bat, you're not thinking about what you had for breakfast or who you argued with last night. Your entire focus is on getting in the right mindset for your at bat. You're not thinking about how you can add to your stats. You're preparing, envisioning your swing. It's time to think about bringing your teammates on the bases home, getting the runs batted in. You're visualizing the game you're playing today, not yesterday or tomorrow. And then, when you focus on serving others, your state of mind improves, regardless of your individual stats. That's a win-win."

> "When you can control your mindset, you won't feel like every conversation is a battle."

Sam mulled that over for a moment, then asked, "What would a win-lose look like in that game?"

"That, my friend, would be if you decided to focus on your ambition at your team's expense. Sure, you might get your home run or whatever, but the team lost. Only a selfish knucklehead would do that."

Sam laughed. "Careful, Mike. You're talking to this year's chief knucklehead."

"Nah, I know you're not setting up win-lose situations just to be a jerk. Like I said, you have to go into every interaction with the mindset that you want to build trust so that each person gets at least part of what they want or need. Then, you'll win as a team."

"Sounds good, but how is that going to work? It feels like everything is coming at me and it all feels urgent. I can't stop and make sure everyone's happy. The only way I can survive is to keep moving."

Mike drank the last of his coffee. "Tell you what. Why don't you try this for a week? Each morning, when you wake up, make a conscious choice to look for the win-win in all your conversations. Think of everyone you talk to as a member of your team. Ask yourself how you can help the team today. When you can control your mindset, you won't feel like every conversation is a battle."

"Well, you took the time to sit down and talk to me. The least I can do is try it. By the way, what do you call this mindset thing?"

Mike pushed back his chair and stood up. "Well, some people would call it being Win Some or having a win-win mindset." He grinned at Sam, "But for this year's official knucklehead, let's call it *Grab Your Bat.*"

This time it was Sam who laughed out loud.

Mike knocked his knuckles gently on the table in farewell. "Come see me when you're ready for more Win Some secrets." Then he turned and walked out of the coffee shop, leaving Sam to think about what he'd heard.

> A Win Some mindset leads to win-win relationships.

A Win Some mindset leads to win-win relationships. Sam thought he'd better *grab his bat* before heading home to Ethan. He wasn't sure what he'd just agreed to, but he would try this win-win idea just to see if it helped at home. Things couldn't get much worse.

CHAPTER TEN

SUCCESSFUL SINGLE

The next morning, Sam lingered in his bedroom while he thought about how and when to try Mike's advice. Why not start with Ethan? Lord knows he had a stadium-sized well of trust to build in his relationship with his son.

Mike said to manage my mindset first thing. Sam paced his bedroom, wishing he'd asked more questions the previous night. Finally, he decided to sit on his bed, close his eyes, and see if he could picture what a Win Some conversation with his son would look.

In less than a minute, he was tapping his foot on the floor. Maybe if he squinched his eyes? So far, all he could think of were the arguments and icy silences over the months since Aileen had died. That wasn't helping. Sam moved up to sit against the headboard with his legs stretched in front of him. He took a deep breath and closed his eyes again. Immediately he was reliving the scene at the grocery store, arguing with Ethan over the case of energy drinks. His eyes popped open. *Don't go there.*

He pulled his legs close and crisscrossed them. Every thought in his head focused on all the times he'd tried and failed. Then it hit him that he wasn't using the technique Mike had described. If he could learn how to tune out everything that didn't matter when he picked up the bat—and he had, years ago at the start of his career— then he wasn't going to let his past faults keep him from his goal this morning.

This time when Sam closed his eyes, he saw himself picking up his favorite bat. He gave it a couple of swings to warm up. Then he found that place in his mind where he set his goal for each at bat. It felt quiet, yet deep, as if it were waiting for something to fill it. All he needed to do today was create one Win Some connection. That would prove to him that this mindset thing would work. He reminded himself it had taken months of practice to reach the point where he could step into his game mindset as soon as he picked up his bat.

And that's the moment that shifted his thoughts. Sam could see that one conversation with his son. Well, he hoped it would be a conversation. But he was going to start with something that could be a win for them.

He didn't exactly leap off the bed, but he felt a ripple of hope. With more excitement than he'd experienced in months, he finished dressing and left his room.

> All he needed to do today was create one Win Some connection.

When he reached the kitchen, there was no sign of Ethan. Maybe he was sleeping late during his spring break. Or he was still avoiding his dad. Either way, this wasn't exactly how Sam pictured his Win Some moment.

He barely had time to wonder if he should wake Ethan so they could talk before his son strolled into the kitchen.

"Hey, buddy, I thought you might be sleeping in today." Sam saw Ethan carrying his school backpack.

"Eddie Hinton called to see if I could spend the day at his house. His mom is going to text you and all that. And she said she'd pick me up at eight o'clock this morning and bring me home this afternoon, so you don't have to spend time driving back and forth." Ethan slung the backpack under his chair before grabbing an orange from the bowl on the table.

"Do I know Mrs. Hinton? That name doesn't sound familiar." Sam checked his phone to see if he'd missed the woman's text. Nothing there. "You know I have to meet your friends' parents if you're going to their house."

Ethan frowned. Then he shrugged before continuing to peel his orange over a plate. "Oh, yeah, Eddie's mom is Mrs. Sublett because she and Eddie's dad got divorced, and she got married again." He watched his father move around the kitchen with his peripheral vision.

"I still don't know this woman. Where does she live, and what are you guys planning to do all day?" Sam put a toasted bagel covered with peanut butter in front of his son, who made a face. "Eat it. You need more than fruit." As he turned back to the stove and set a skillet on a burner, he asked over his shoulder, "Why haven't I heard about your plan for today before right now?"

"'Cause Eddie didn't invite me until this morning. His mom works and doesn't allow him to have someone there while she's gone. But she's working from home today, so she said it was okay." Ethan devoured his bagel between sentences. "Come on, Dad, it's really boring around here with you gone most of the day. And Eddie's mom is nice. She won't let us get in trouble."

Sam stared at the empty skillet for a few moments, realizing this was his opportunity to create a Win Some moment with his son.

"If I meet your friend's mom and get her to promise that you'll not leave her property until she brings you home, you can go."

Ethan did a fist pump behind his father's back. When Sam sat across the table, his son tried not to show his excitement.

"What do you boys have planned for the day?"

"Just working on some computer games. Nothin' special." Ethan shrugged.

Sam watched his son, not entirely sure the boy was telling him everything. But he decided to avoid the possibility of an argument. They were finally talking.

"Well, if Mrs. Sublett is going to text me, she'd better do it soon. It's ten minutes to eight." Once again, Sam lifted his phone to verify the woman hadn't reached out.

A horn beeped in the driveway.

Ethan raced to the kitchen window. "It's them. Come on, Dad, please? I really want to go today."

Sam looked at the boy who was growing up so fast. His child's face was taking on the contours of a young man. Ethan was already inching toward the door. Sam held up his hand to keep him in place.

"I'll go outside with you and meet Mrs. Sublett. If I agree to this, you must promise you'll do what she says, and you'll be home no later than five o'clock tonight. And you won't leave their house to go anywhere else."

By the look on Ethan's face, Sam knew his son had expected him to refuse. Now the boy's face lit up with relief. "Okay, I promise, Dad. You won't regret this."

"One other thing."

Some of the light faded from the boy's eyes. "What?"

"You have to remember one thing."

"What's that?"

"I love you, Son."

Sam almost didn't hear the reply when his boy mumbled, "Yeah, me too."

Throwing his arm over his son's shoulder, he opened the door. "Let's go meet your hostess so you guys can get started on your day."

They walked out together with Sam full of gratitude for the peaceful moment he'd just shared with his son. Maybe Mike was on to something.

CHAPTER ELEVEN

ON A ROLL

On his way home that evening, Sam was deep in thought. First, he considered the morning's conversation with Ethan. It had felt wonderful to start the day without an argument. Ethan hadn't rolled his eyes once. That had set the tone for the rest of Sam's day.

Sam made an effort to say good morning to the players in the locker room when he arrived. The terse nods he received in return were better than the razzing he got the day before, he supposed. Before joining Anker on the field, he was careful to picture the two of them getting along: Sam sharing his batting knowledge and Anker putting it into practice without wincing every time Sam spoke.

Their interaction hadn't been great, but it was an improvement over their first day working together. Sam thought he was getting the hang of being Win Some. Mike would be proud of him.

He pulled into the garage and leaped out of the car, eager to continue his earlier conversation with Ethan. Sam had a mental image of his son waiting in the kitchen for his arrival. They'd talk about their day while making supper together before tossing a few pitches around in the backyard.

> It had felt wonderful to start the day without an argument.

But his son wasn't waiting for him. His backpack hung on the arm of the couch. Raucous music blasted from overhead, shaking the pictures on the shelves in the family room. Ethan was home, but he was in his room.

So much for fanciful notions that his son was as eager to reconnect as Sam was. Evidently, Sam's concession in letting Ethan spend the day with his friend didn't mean as much to the boy as it did to the father.

Drooping a bit at the letdown, Sam made his way up to Ethan's room. After knocking and receiving no answer, he opened the door.

Ethan looked up from his laptop and scowled but did nothing to lower the volume of the music shaking the room. Sam walked over to the stereo and did it for him.

"How did your day go with Eddie?"

"What do you care?" That was a definite sneer on his son's face.

"Of course I care. I came up here as soon as I got home to hear all about it. Did you get in a fight with your friend?" Sam couldn't understand Ethan's change in attitude from morning to evening.

"No, we didn't fight. Which you would have known if you had been here when Mrs. Sublett brought me home. You said I had to be here by five. I thought that meant you'd be here too. But it's after seven, and I didn't even know when you were coming home."

Sam's heart dropped. He'd messed up again. "I'm so sorry. I didn't realize you'd think I would be here when you got home. I'll do better next time."

"Sure, whatever." His son stubbornly kept his eyes on the laptop screen.

Not knowing what else to do, Sam sat on the end of the bed. "I am here now. And I honestly am interested in what you and Eddie did today. Why don't you come downstairs with me? We can talk while I make some mac and cheese with ham." If he had to bribe his son with one of the boy's favorite comfort foods, that's what he would do.

"I'm not hungry."

"Come on, Ethan. I'm sorry I worried you. I thought we had a good morning and could talk about your plans for the rest of your break tonight. And maybe watch a movie after we eat. You can pick." *Way to pile on the bribes, Sam*, he thought. But he would do anything to see the enthusiasm his son's face had reflected earlier that day.

Ethan looked up. "Yeah? Maybe *Guardians of the Galaxy* and then *Volume 2*?"

"I think we can make that work since you don't have to get up early for school."

"Okay, let me finish what I'm working on. I'll be down in a few minutes." Ethan turned back to the laptop.

"See you in a few." Sam pulled the door shut behind him as he left the room. He wondered what Ethan found so interesting on that laptop but didn't want to break their fragile truce. And he could use the time before Ethan followed him to the kitchen to *grab his bat* again. He needed to regain the focus he'd found that morning.

"Hey, Dad! Can you put some extra ham in the mac? And some of those sliced black olives?" Ethan hollered from his room.

"You got it. Come and get it soon, or I'll feed it to the ducks." Sam reached the bottom of the steps, hopeful once again that the two of them would have a Win Some evening. Tomorrow he'd make sure to find Mike and get some reinforcement to help him maintain his Grab-Your-Bat focus.

CHAPTER TWELVE

THE ON-DECK CIRCLE

Sam arrived at training camp early the next morning and went looking for Mike.

"There you are. I've been about five minutes behind you since I got here." Sam strode into the laundry room where the clubbie was shaking out towels before folding them. Out of habit, Sam grabbed a towel, folded it, and placed it in the growing pile on the table.

"Well, you've found me now. What can I do for you?" Mike looked at the careful folds in the towel Sam had handled and pushed a heap of them toward him. "I see someone's trained you right."

"Yeah, Aileen made sure I knew how to do my share of the housework. We had some good talks while folding laundry."

"Well, I'm always happy for the help, and open to a good talk. What's on your mind?" Mike opened the door of a dryer, lowering the noise level in the room. He pulled the load out to add to the pile they were working on.

"First, I wanted to let you know I tried being Win Some with Ethan yesterday morning."

"And how did that go?" Mike paused to pay attention to Sam's reply.

"Well, we talked before I left to come to work. He wanted to spend the day with a friend, but I didn't know the kid's parents. The boy's mother was supposedly going to text me for permission to pick Ethan up but didn't. Before you told me about grabbing my bat, I would have shut him down and told him he had to stay home. But I could tell he really wanted to go. Anyway, when the kid and his mother showed up, it turned out she'd dropped her phone and broken it that morning. That was when her son asked her to text me. So, I talked with her for a few minutes until I felt comfortable that she'd be there keeping an eye on the boys. And I let Ethan spend the day with his friend."

"Sounds like you made some progress. What did you get out of that situation?"

"Well, I didn't leave the house with my son angry at me. And I was able to make him happy by approving his plans." Sam started another pile of towels.

"Was that what you wanted for your win?" Mike stacked laundry baskets, beginning to clean up the area while the last dryer finished its load.

"It was so much better than fighting or Ethan not speaking to me that it felt like a win. I know it wasn't a big win, but I was grateful for the small one. And I did get the reassurance I needed by meeting his friend's mom before they went off together. Without an argument, I might add."

"Did you use your Grab-Your-Bat technique anywhere else?"

"So, I said hello to several of the guys and didn't shut down when they just grunted in return. And I don't know if I can say I accomplished anything with Anker, but the kid didn't jump every time I said something to him. I thought about how you said Grab Your Bat is all about framing how I can help the team. I know I still have a lot of work to do on that, but I wanted to let you know I tried, and I did see some changes in the people around me."

Mike laughed and slapped Sam on the shoulder. "And maybe they saw a change in you, Sam. I'm glad you tried the first step. You're right, though, it takes constant practice, being vigilant about maintaining the mental focus on what's going to help your team. But you already do that in the game

> "It takes constant practice, being vigilant about maintaining the mental focus on what's going to help your team."

every day. Now you're learning to take that focus with you when you leave the field. You're going to be amazed at what you can do with it at home and with your friends."

"Well, if I didn't believe you before, I do now. You said that Grab Your Bat is just the first step. You mean there's more to learn?" Sam grabbed one of the towering towel stacks and loaded it onto the cart Mike pushed up to the table.

"Meet me for lunch in the cafeteria and I'll tell you more. And thanks for the help." Mike shoved the cart out the door. "Turn off the lights, will ya?"

* * *

Sam could hardly wait for lunchtime. If Mike knew other methods he could use to reconnect with his son, he was ready to learn.

He waited impatiently for Mike to go through the line and look around. Sam waved at the clubbie who made his way across the room, exchanging cheerful greetings with everyone he passed.

"Okay, Mike. Spill your secrets." Sam grinned to show he was teasing despite the commanding tone.

The clubbie took a big bite of his roast beef sandwich, chewed, and swallowed before answering. "You're right. There are more steps to being a Win Some person. But you'll want to take them one at a time."

"Why's that? If there are several more steps I need, why not tell me all of them right now?" Sam dropped his spoon into the empty soup bowl on his tray, distracted from his meal by the need to hear what Mike was about to reveal.

"When you first learned baseball, did you start swinging at balls on your first day? Or did you practice how to grip the bat until you were certain you could hit the ball without losing the bat? Does a pitcher start learning his skill by throwing screwballs, or does he begin by pitching straight over the plate?"

"The second, I guess." A big gulp of iced tea helped Sam think about why Mike was asking these basic questions.

"That's right. You learned how to hold the bat, then how to stand in the box, and so on, until you were ready to put all the steps together and face a pitcher. You learn to be Win Some in the same way. You know the first step…" Mike paused and pointed at Sam.

"Oh, yeah, Grab Your Bat."

"Correct. And you've practiced a little bit. I can see you're eager to go deeper, so I'm going to share the next step. But you have to promise you won't shirk practicing the first step until it becomes so natural you don't even have to think about it."

Sam crossed his heart and held up his right hand with the first three fingers raised and his thumb holding down the little finger. "Scout's honor."

Mike smiled. "You were a Boy Scout? That fits."

"Eight years."

Mike finished his sandwich and wiped his mouth.

"Okay. Here's the second step to Win Some. You want to take notes?"

Mike watched Sam's eyes widen while he patted his pockets searching for paper and something to write with. He laughed and held up a hand to stop Sam from jumping up to search for writing tools.

"Just joking. But these steps do give you a lot to think about. That's another reason you shouldn't try to jump into all of them at once. They build on each other, and each makes you stronger in mind and attitude."

"Okay. I get that. So, what do you suggest for my next step? I want to make even more headway with Ethan and Anker. And my dad too. But maybe I'll have the guts to try this out with strangers before I face him." Sam was only half kidding about facing his dad. He'd always wanted his father's approval but resented the need to ask for it. He hoped the Win Some tactic would change that dynamic.

> "All the mental and physical preparation around how you can help the team gets distilled in the present moment."

"Step two is controlling your thoughts and actions today because you can't control the past. It's Controlling the Controllables!"

"Sounds easy, but I bet you're going to tell me there's a lot more to it than just thinking positive thoughts."

Mike nodded, "That's right. Let's call this step the On-Deck Circle. We're going back to baseball analogies because you have those at the tips of your fingers. In the on-deck circle, the batter is aware of everything about the game situation in that moment. You know how many runners are on base. You know how close the infielders are, the number of outs, the type of pitcher you are facing, and how deep the outfielders play. You're not thinking about how you missed a fastball down the middle on your last at bat, or how someone scraped your car in the parking lot. You're taking that Grab-Your-Bat focus and bringing it to the batter's box for this moment. This at bat is your chance to help your team, to help others. That's where your control sits—in the present. All the mental and physical preparation around *how* you can help the team gets distilled in the present moment."

"Wow. You're good at explaining this, you know?"

That drew a chuckle from Mike. "One day you'll be just as good. It didn't come like a flash of lightning to me. It took time to learn each step and figure out how to apply it to my life. All I can tell you is that someday you'll reach the point where it's a part of you. You have the will to do this, Sam. I can tell you want to be a Win Some person with your son and father, and even with your teammates and fans. Don't let life control you. Take control of how you react. That's a big step."

Mike stood and collected his tray. "Don't let this overwhelm you. Remember: one day at a time. One step at a time. Let me know how it goes or if you have questions. I'm in your corner. Or should I say, I'm here to help you knock it out of the park?"

> "Don't let life control you. Take control of how you react."

"Thanks, Mike. I appreciate your time and wisdom. I won't forget this, man. And I'll be sure to report how fast I'm earning my Mr. Congeniality sash." Sam waved goodbye to the clubbie who'd given him so much to think about again. Every time he'd talked to Mike during this spring training, Sam felt like he came away with homework that would improve his life. And he was ready to get back to work, mentally and physically.

CHAPTER THIRTEEN

LEFT ON BASE

Ethan had left the milk out again. Last week, heck, two days ago, Sam would have yelled at the boy for that. This morning he stopped to think about how he could turn Ethan's forgetfulness into a win-win for the family team. He would practice grabbing his bat and then step into the on-deck circle before he said anything.

Ethan had been hinting about home-cooked meals for a while now. Sam wondered if he could come up with a way to make that happen while getting his son to focus on what he was supposed to be doing to help out. Sam didn't have a lot of time that morning, so he went looking for Ethan.

He found the boy in the family room, once again engrossed in typing away on his laptop.

"Hey, can you put that down for a minute? I want to talk to you about something." Sam didn't take a seat because he knew he had to get moving if he was going to be on time for his practice session with Anker.

"Yeah, what about?" Ethan didn't lay the laptop aside but did stop typing to look up at his father. "Then can I talk to you about something important?"

"I don't have time this morning. Can it wait until I get home?" Sam wanted to stay focused on his effort to get Ethan to be more responsible before he had to leave for work.

"Not really. It's about Grandpop. We've been video chatting, and there's something wrong with that place where he's staying."

"Look, Ethan. I know your grandfather isn't happy with anything right now. He's made it clear he doesn't like the facility I found for him, but he'll complete his rehab before you know it, and then he can go back home to Minnesota." Sam's resolution to have a conversation with his son was getting sidetracked by his anger over what he saw as his father using Ethan to make his complaints known.

"No, Dad! That's not what's going on. Just listen for a minute. I think something is happening—"

"There's nothing wrong except an old man trying his best to make everyone around him as miserable as he is. But I don't have time to listen to him rant and rave every day about how he hates being there. It's not like he's alone or that we've deserted him. We're over there all the time."

> Sam's resolution to have a conversation with his son was getting sidetracked by his anger.

"You didn't even give me a chance to tell you what he said. You're not being fair." Ethan scowled at his father. "You don't have time to listen to Grandpop, and you don't have time to spend with me. I don't even know why you're still here. The only thing you're interested in is your stupid baseball career. Well, I hate baseball. And I hate you too! Mom would at least listen, and she'd understand."

Ethan jumped to his feet and stormed up the stairs. Sam tracked his son's arrival in his bedroom by the sound of the slamming door.

Glancing at his watch, he debated whether he had time to run up the stairs and call the boy out for his behavior. Sam realized if he didn't leave within the next two minutes, he'd be late. This argument was going to have to wait until he got home. If Aileen had to put up with this sort of attitude while he was living out in Las Vegas, he was beginning to understand why she had wanted him to be home more often.

Sam wanted to slam a door or two on his way out of the house and into the garage. He didn't give in to the urge, but he felt so discouraged about his failed On-Deck Circle attempt that he nearly forgot to open the garage door before shifting his SUV into reverse.

Mike had warned him about getting ahead of himself. And now he knew why. Getting cocky because he got Grab Your Bat right the first few times he used it had led to tearing down all the trust he'd built with Ethan in the past week.

As he pulled into the parking lot at the stadium, Sam realized the milk was still sitting on the kitchen counter.

CHAPTER FOURTEEN

EYE ON THE BALL

"I messed up so bad, Mike. I don't know if Ethan will even speak to me tonight."

Sam ran into the clubbie in the parking lot when they arrived for work at the same time. He'd taken advantage of their walk into the facility to ask Mike if they could sit down and talk sometime that day. They met in the empty bleachers late that afternoon and climbed to seats high above the field.

"There's an easy solve for that problem." Mike leaned back in his seat and crossed his ankles atop the one in front of him.

"I'm glad it looks that way to you. You didn't see the look on his face when Ethan told me he hates baseball, and he hates me." Sam's mood had continued to sour since his encounter with his son earlier that day. He tugged the brim of his cap lower, pretending to shield his eyes from the late afternoon sun. He didn't want his friend to know they were stinging with tears. He didn't pity himself. He felt terrible that he'd, once again, failed his son and, by association, his late wife.

"Okay, buddy. Lay it on me. Where did I go wrong, and how do I make Ethan listen to me?" *May as well tear the bandage straight off,* Sam thought.

"It sounds like you got distracted from your mission. You intended to talk with Ethan about being more responsible for helping around the house. Which means your role was to listen as much as you talked. But as soon as he mentioned your dad, you lost focus. I've noticed that before. What is it about your dad that angers you so?"

"Ha. If I could explain that, I wouldn't need your advice today. I'm not even sure what I'm feeling is anger."

"Well, there's something there that you're going to have to address if that's what keeps you from being Win Some. Why don't you tell me something about your dad? I know he lived up in Minnesota, and that he's here now."

Sam was silent for several minutes, leaning forward with his elbows on his knees. Mike didn't push. The two men watched the activity on the field while Sam thought about how to explain his relationship with Richard Masterson.

His gaze on his clasped hands, Sam finally spoke. "Did I ever tell you my dad's a war hero?"

"No. Sounds like a story there. What did he do?" Mike kept his eyes on the field.

"Yeah, he got drafted for Vietnam. I don't know a lot about his time in service. He never wanted to talk about it. Anyway, I do know there was this one time he was in a big firefight. Dad ended up single-handedly preventing the Viet Cong from overrunning his squad's location. He was wounded three times while saving his buddies. That earned him the Purple Heart. When they returned to base, Dad's commanding officer recommended him for the Distinguished Service Cross."

"Wow. That's incredible. You must be proud of him."

"I am. I don't know if I could ever take risks like that." Sam fell silent again. Then he went on, "I guess that's the problem. I know I'll never do anything as selfless or heroic as Dad has. After he came home from the war, he started a trucking company with one vehicle, making trips from his hometown to the Twin Cities. Now he owns one of the best-known long-haul firms in the Midwest." Sam frowned. "You know, Mike, I always knew I could never live up to my dad. He brought me up to be the man of my family, to make good decisions, and to be a good provider. It didn't matter if it was something I wanted to do or not. He would always tell me, 'Just step up and get it done, Son.' He made it look so easy, figuring out what to do with his life and moving forward all the time. I don't ever remember him second-guessing any decision he made.

"But I struggle to know the best things to do for my family. Every single day. It's always in the back of my mind that I should be doing more, or better, or different. Then, losing Aileen made me realize how many decisions I made that weren't the best for my family. But it's too late to fix that now. I feel like I'm letting everyone down. Dad, Ethan, the team, and even you."

"How could you be letting me down?"

"You took the time to try to show me how to build trust. It's something so simple. And I can't even get that right."

"Sam, I want you to hear two things. One, you could never let me down. It's not your responsibility to make me or anyone else happy. And two, if you're doing your best to take care of your father and your son, you are not letting them down."

Sam removed his cap and rubbed his eyes hard. He slapped the team cap back on his head before facing his friend.

"I just realized something. I want so much to win my father's approval. And Ethan's too. I can't seem to make it work." Sam frowned again. "Does that make me selfish?"

"I don't think so. You know better than anyone how much effort you put into supporting your family and providing what they need. Look at how you moved your dad here so he could be close to family while recuperating from spinal surgery. And it's not selfish to want to have the people you're close to acknowledge what you do. The thing about that is, sometimes they never will. And that's okay." Mike turned so he could watch Sam's eyes. "What you *can* work on is managing your mindset when you don't get approval or appreciation because that is no longer what you are focused on."

"You're talking about the Win Some steps, aren't you? We're back full circle to my fight with Ethan this morning." Sam gave the other man a small smile.

"That's exactly when those steps are most useful. If the person you're communicating with has another agenda, that's when you stay focused on finding a benefit for both of you—a win." Mike gestured to the field where a few of the rookies were taking batting practice. "Out there, when you find yourself distracted during a game, you control your mind, get rid of your doubts, and think like a winner. You practiced for years to lock that training in. And guess what? You're still practicing every day when you show up here. I believe you can take the power of your mind off the field and build a strong, meaningful relationship with anyone you choose. Now *you* have to choose to believe it."

Sam watched the men on the field for a moment. He turned to shake hands with the clubbie. "You're right. I choose to believe I can grab my bat and step into the on-deck circle of my life. And I don't need to wait for anyone's approval before I begin. Thank you, my friend."

"My pleasure. Let me ask you, do I have your permission to pray for you and your family?"

"What, talk to some old guy in a white robe in the sky? You know I don't believe in any of that stuff." Sam shook his head in disgust.

"I told you before that I'm not asking you to do anything except focus on the Win Some mindset. However, you know I believe in something bigger than myself, a God who loves me and helps me. I rely on those prayers for everything in my life. That's just how I roll."

"Well, if you put it that way, I guess it can't hurt. Just don't expect that I'm going to go to a Bible study or anything like that with you. Your faith is your business, and I'll thank you for leaving me out of it."

> "You can take the power of your mind off the field and build a strong, meaningful relationship with anyone you choose."

Mike grinned. "I'm always here if you need to talk to me again. And I can always use some experienced help with the never-ending towel situation."

For the first time that day, Sam laughed, and it felt like a weight lifted from his shoulders.

CHAPTER FIFTEEN

AT BAT

Three days after talking to Mike, Sam and Ethan had constructed another shaky truce. Spring break was over, so Ethan was back in school. That left them with less time to spend together. Sam thought that wasn't a bad thing at this point, as long as they weren't fighting. He did feel better about his interactions with his teammates. He'd gone out of his way to strike up conversations with players he'd been close to before his move to Las Vegas, and he made a point of greeting the newer guys. That had led to some joking around and light banter in the locker room. What he most enjoyed in getting reacquainted with the team was hearing about their families and lives outside the stadium. Some of their stories made him realize he wasn't the only person struggling to balance baseball and family life.

"Hey, Sam! How's it going?" Mike said as he entered the locker room, late that afternoon.

Sam's phone rang. He was smiling at Mike as he pulled it from his pocket.

"Sam Masterson here."

Mike turned to signal he was going to leave but stopped when Sam's face tightened.

"I see. And where is that?" A short pause ensued before Sam said, "Thank you. I'll be there as soon as possible."

"What's wrong? You look awful. Is it your father? Or Ethan?"

"I can't believe this. Ethan's in jail for assaulting someone at the rehab center, and Dad was involved somehow. He's on his way to the hospital." Sam yanked his locker door open and grabbed his wallet and watch. "I've got to get out of here. I have no idea what happened, but I've got to go take care of my family."

"Okay. The most important thing right now is to find out what's wrong with your dad. Ethan's safe where he is." Mike was at Sam's side as they pushed past a handful of players coming in from the showers. "I'm coming with you if only to remind you to stay Win Some to make it easier to get the details."

"You think this is the right time for Win Some?" Sam sounded bitter and disappointed.

"There was never a more crucial time than now."

Sam stopped at his car and looked across it at his friend. "You'd better be right, Mike. Because I don't know how to begin to fix this for either of them."

Twenty minutes later, Sam and Mike strode through the emergency entrance and approached the information desk.

"My father arrived from the Bayou Rehabilitation Resident Center by ambulance. I need to see him and speak to his doctor."

The woman behind the counter didn't even look up. "Name?"

"Richard Masterson. The rehab center told me he was injured but didn't give me any details."

She typed onto a tablet for a few seconds. "He's here. How did you say you're related to Mr. Masterson?"

"I'm his son. Look, can I see him, please?" The drive to the hospital had given Mike time to talk Sam down from his first flush of anger and anxiety.

"Not yet, sir. The doctor is with him now. In the meantime, I need his health insurance information and medical history." The woman still hadn't raised her eyes from the tablet.

"The rehab center has all that information. Why haven't you received it from them?" Sam was confused. The rehabilitation center had required copies of his dad's health history, surgeries, and insurance information for their files. If his dad was here, where was his advocate from the facility?

"I don't know the answer to that, sir. We have none of his information on file yet. If you can just have a seat, fill out these forms, and sign them, that will help your father." She pressed a key on her tablet, and a printer on the corner of the desk spit out several pages. "Do you need a pen?" She gave the two men a bored glance as she handed Sam the papers.

"At least tell me if Bayou Rehabilitation sent someone with my dad. The patients are supposed to have health advocates accompany them in case something like this happens." Sam looked at the woman's name badge. "Charlene, if no one came from Bayou with my dad, I really should be in there with him."

"Sorry, sir. You'll have to take a seat and wait for the doctor to finish his examination. I'll let the nurses know you're waiting. Someone will come to get you when they can. What's your name?"

Mike saw Sam's frustration and gave him a gentle elbow nudge. "That sounds like a good plan, Sam. The doctors will need your dad's health history. The sooner you fill out those forms, the better care they can give him."

Sam grudgingly accepted that he couldn't see his dad until he crossed all the t's and dotted all the i's the hospital demanded. "Fine. My name's Sam Masterson. I'll be waiting right over there," he pointed to a line of chairs closest to the swinging doors leading to the exam rooms, "and please have the nurses tell my dad that I'm here."

"Sure." Charlene turned her attention to the tablet, effectively dismissing the two men before her desk.

"What's going on, Mike? Where's the rehab center advocate? I chose that place specifically because they offered that service—someone to stay with their patients until family arrives if they need medical care. It sounds like they just put my dad into an ambulance and waved goodbye." Sam wasn't only worried about his dad's health; he was livid that the people he'd entrusted Richard's care to ignored their obligation. "They'd better have an explanation for why he's here in the emergency room, and especially why he's alone. I don't understand why family members can't be in the room during examinations. Someone had better come out here and give me some answers."

"All valid questions. But we're in someone else's stadium right now. And they get to make the rules. The best thing you can do is meet their expectations and focus on what your dad needs." Mike drew a pen from an inside pocket of his warmup jacket and handed it to the younger man.

Sam shook his head. "You don't get it. I may be mad at my dad half the time, but I love him, and I'm afraid that something serious happened today. No one seems to know anything." He focused on the prepared list of health questions, checking off the ones that applied to his father.

The two men were quiet for a few minutes while Sam finished the paperwork. He scrawled his signature at the bottom of the last page. "Do you think they'll change their mind once they have the means to bill him for his treatment?"

"Cynical. But it can't hurt."

Mike watched Sam walk the papers to the desk and hand them to Charlene.

Once Sam sat down beside him again, Mike began, "I get that you're facing a tough situation right now. It can't hurt to give you the third Win Some lesson so you can ease through this instead of making it harder for both you and your dad. If you can remember to be Win Some, you'll get better results. Nothing good ever happens when the patient's family causes a stink. You don't want to detract attention from your dad's care. You want everyone on his side. And then, you can use this technique again when we go to get Ethan out of jail."

"Oh, no." Sam covered his face with his hands. "I'd almost forgotten that he's waiting for me too. How the heck could Ethan pull some stunt and get himself arrested at the same time his grandpop got injured? You don't suppose he's the reason Dad's in here, do you?"

"You won't know until you can talk to them. And that's another reason for learning this At-Bat technique before those conversations happen. You'll need every tool you can muster to keep everyone talking without losing their tempers."

"Okay. You're right. At this moment, I'm furious with Ethan for putting himself in a situation that led to him getting arrested. I'm afraid of what that means for his future. And I don't know whether to be angry at Dad for possibly being involved in Ethan's mess or worried that he's seriously hurt."

"Alright. You're At Bat right now." Mike tapped Sam's shoulder as if tagging him in.

"Okay, looks like we're going to have plenty of time for me to learn everything you're ready to teach me today." The waiting room was half full of family members waiting to hear about loved ones. Occasionally, nurses or doctors came through the doors, called out a patient's name, and then spoke to the people waiting for updates. Sam's chair faced the doors head-on. He was taking no chances that he'd miss hearing his father's name.

Mike thought for a moment and then said, "Think about being in the batter's box. You scope out the field, try to determine the pitcher's strategy, and check the runners. You look for weak spots. You assess the situation and decide how you want to swing when the pitch comes at you. Maybe you take a few pitches. What do you do when you get a couple of strikes?"

Sam replied quickly, "I usually step out of the box and figure out why the pitcher is getting one over on me."

"That's right. When you realize that something isn't going according to plan, you step out, regrip your bat, and make some adjustments. It's the same in relationships. Sometimes when you are trying to have a positive conversation, things go wrong. The other person might get mad and back away or say something you weren't expecting. Rather than striking out, take a minute to regrip, change your approach, and then try again."

"Step three sounds complicated." Sam groused.

"Well, it can be." Mike agreed. "You can't always predict what the pitcher is going to do, or what might happen on the field. You've got to pay attention to everything around you and adjust moment by moment. Part of that regripping process is managing your anger when things don't go the way you want them to."

"I guess I'm trying to figure out what kind of pitch I'm going to get and spot any weak spots on the field where I could sink the ball, so I can get a hit."

Mike replied, "That's right, your goal is to get a hit, so you assess the situation, choose an approach, and then swing. During a game, you vary your swing depending on the pitch and where you want to land the ball. It's the same thing in relationships; you vary your approach depending on the situation and what you want to achieve. I don't want to make you feel bad, but can we talk about the grocery store incident?"

Sam groaned and put his head in his hands. "Oh, man! I didn't read that situation well at all. I was so focused on myself that I ignored how the clerk must have felt when I was so condescending in front of all those people. I embarrassed her, then I embarrassed Ethan... I didn't plan for it to turn out that way at all."

"So, let's use that experience as an example of what not to do. Now that you know about being At Bat, how could you have approached the situation winsomely?" Mike looked Sam straight in the eyes and waited for his answer.

After a long pause, Sam looked at his hands and said, "Well, I could have been gracious when Darla recognized me instead of biting her head off. And I could have chosen not to correct Ethan in a public place."

Mike leaned over and bumped his shoulder into Sam's. "See, you've got this! A big part of being Win Some is making smart choices about the emotional tone you use with people. If your goal is to connect with them so you can have a win-win conversation about what you both want, then you have to choose the right tone. In some situations, you may want to be respectful, in others you may want to be the confident professional, and sometimes you may need to show your vulnerability."

Sam reared back in his seat. "Vulnerable? You want me to be weak? How does that help me win?"

Mike laid a hand on Sam's arm. "Whoa, buddy, I didn't say anything about being weak. Being vulnerable requires a great deal of strength. When you are vulnerable, you are brave enough to be open and speak from your heart. That is a courageous position to take."

"I hear you, but this feels like a lot to take in right now. What if I get it wrong and make things worse for Dad and Ethan? Sometimes my temper gets the best of me." Sam wasn't sure he was ready to trust his skill at the techniques Mike had taught him when the people in danger were so important to him.

Mike shook his head. "When you're at bat, you continually reassess and recalibrate. If you strike on the first pitch, you try something different on the next one. Remember those times when the catcher starts getting under your skin and you lose focus? What do you do then?"

Sam replied quickly, "I step out of the batter's box and take a couple swings to regrip and get my head back in the game."

"There you go, Slammin' Sam!" Mike nodded and smiled. "When you start talking with someone and you feel yourself getting mad or think your approach isn't creating a positive connection, you gotta regrip. You can do that by taking a deep breath, thinking about creating a Win Some situation, and then choosing how you want to react. Instead of letting emotions cloud your thinking so you do or say something you regret, you stay in control and decide on the best approach. Sorry to say this, but you have the perfect opportunity to practice that emotional control right here." Mike winked and nodded his head toward Charlene.

> "When you're at bat, you continually reassess and recalibrate."

CHAPTER SIXTEEN

EMOTIONS IN CHECK

Suddenly, the outside doors hissed open. A tall, scowling woman walked in. Looking neither right nor left, she headed straight to the information desk. She walked like someone used to giving orders and watching everyone jump.

Sam and Mike observed her interaction with the information clerk. The woman rapped her knuckles on the desk to demand Charlene's attention. She did most of the talking, pointing her finger and shaking her head in disagreement with whatever Charlene told her. When the clerk motioned toward the chairs where Sam and Mike waited, the woman slowly turned to make her own observation.

"Looks like I'm really At Bat now, Mike. That woman is Felicia Young, the CEO of Bayou Rehab. I think she's looking for me." Sam stood and straightened his shoulders, watching the woman stride in his direction.

"Mr. Masterson. I am Felicia Young, CEO of the Bayou Center."

Sam extended his hand. "I remember meeting you, Ms. Young, when I brought my father to your facility. This is my friend, Mike Gilchrist."

Ms. Young eyed Sam's hand for a second too long, before reluctantly putting her hand in it for a quick shake. She pointedly ignored Mike, who shrugged and resumed his seat. She also didn't invite them to use her first name, but Sam decided not to test her.

"Have you any idea how hard it is for me to get away from my duties to come here and take care of this debacle?" Ms. Young ignored the chair Sam pulled over for her.

That was a strange approach for someone responsible for the care and safety of their clients. But Sam was more interested in discovering how his father ended up in the hospital. Right now, he needed to be smart and manage his emotions. He could address her attitude later.

"Perhaps you can clarify the situation for me, Ms. Young? I've only heard that my father was injured and brought here for medical attention." Sam figured mentioning Ethan would only interfere with the first item on his agenda: making sure his father would be alright.

> Right now, he needed to be smart and manage his emotions. He could address her attitude later.

"Well, Mr. Masterson was certainly at the center of the incident. And we cannot condone that sort of behavior at Bayou."

Sam felt his temper rise. Taken on top of her unpleasant attitude, if the rehab center was blaming his father for getting hurt, he and Ms. Young might have nothing further to say to each other.

Mike hummed something beneath his breath while flipping through a magazine he'd picked up from a side table. But Sam heard his friend's words.

"Hey, batter, batter, hey!"

Sam mentally shook his shoulders, regripped, and took a practice swing before turning back to the rehab center's rep.

A briefcase-carrying man rushed through the door. Ms. Young raised one imperious finger that caught his attention. He reached her side in several long strides.

"You're late." She didn't look at the new arrival. "This is Bayou's attorney, Wendell Hambleton. Wen, this is Mr. Masterson's son, Sam Masterson."

Sam saw recognition cross the lawyer's eyes, but after a quick sideglance at the CEO's severe face, the man closed his mouth and shook Sam's hand.

"And this is my friend, Mike Gilchrist." Sam made a point of drawing Mike into the conversation.

The lawyer nodded and shook hands with Mike.

"Since I don't have any idea yet what happened to my dad, I have to ask why you think it's necessary to have your attorney here." Sam had an uneasy feeling about their intent.

"It's standard procedure when someone in our care sustains an injury, Mr. Masterson. Why don't we all sit down, and Ms. Young can fill in the details for you." Hambleton pulled a chair around to face the ones where Sam and Mike had been waiting.

Ms. Young inspected the seat of the chair Sam had offered earlier before perching on the edge as if afraid of contracting some disease from a previous occupant.

"Mr. Masterson, your father, Mr. Masterson... oh, this is awkward. May I call you Junior, so we know which Mr. Masterson we're talking about?" Her teeth barely showed in her tight smile.

He gritted his teeth, took a deep breath, and decided he'd match her insincere tone with firmness. "No, you may not. You can call me Sam. And you may use my father's given name, which is Richard."

Felicia Young sighed in exasperation.

What was her game? The woman seemed to be trying to make Sam angry. He glanced at Mike and found his friend entirely focused on the conversation.

"Sam, then." She fastidiously straightened the hem of her skirt before continuing. "The situation is that your son assaulted one of our attendants. He also pushed your father to the floor. Richard was incoherent and injured. Of course, we immediately had him brought here for examination. We also called the police to arrest your son and remove him from our premises." Felicia picked a loose thread off her sleeve as she spoke. "You understand, of course, that we absolutely prohibit such behavior in our facility. Your son, should he be released from jail, is no longer allowed at Bayou."

Sam couldn't believe what he was hearing. Ethan would never hurt his grandfather. He doubted the boy would attack anyone without provocation. But he couldn't blurt that out and set the two rehab center representatives on the defensive.

"And my father?"

"Yes, he has his share of blame for what happened. He was warned several times about refusing to do what the attendants ask, for being recalcitrant and rude. According to the attendant, your father was swearing at him and trying to hit him with his walker." Felicia Young paused and looked directly at Sam. "Perhaps this sort of attitude and behavior runs in the family."

He knew she was referring to the infamous grocery store video. Sam felt his face flush and his temper flare.

Mike spoke up, his voice casual and even. "That seems out of character for the boy I know. It sure would help if we knew what was going on when the incident happened. And I'm positive you didn't intentionally attempt to pressure Sam into talking about anything to do with his son or father without his lawyer present." He gave both Bayou representatives a flat stare that said he was on to them.

The lawyer broke first, dropping his eyes to fuss with the clasp on his briefcase. Felicia Young glared at the man before turning her shoulder to him.

Sam had been about to ask which attendant his son had allegedly assaulted. He was grateful for his friend's calm support and the reminder that he should let his lawyer ask the questions. That is, once he found one not associated with the Millers. Using a team lawyer would only draw attention to the issue and alert the press. If they got wind of this, Sam's name would be in the news again. Sutton would probably fire him.

The swinging doors opened again, and this time it was his father's name a young doctor called. At his side, a tall, broad police officer eyed the little group who turned to acknowledge the doctor's presence.

Sam stepped forward and introduced himself to the doctor whose nameplate read "Connor Bowen." He noticed Mike managed to plant himself firmly between Sam and the people from Bayou. The lawyer introduced Felicia Young and himself to the doctor.

"Mr. Masterson, why don't you come back and see your father while I tell you how he's doing?" Doctor Bowen didn't include anyone else in the invitation, although Felicia did her best to push through the doors behind Sam. The officer pulled the door shut, leaving her outside.

The officer stopped Sam before they reached the examination room, where Doctor Bowen waited outside the door.

"Mr. Masterson, your son hasn't been transferred to the juvenile facility yet. We're holding him at the police station for now. You'll need to talk to the other responding officers, Sergeant Mahew and Officer Grant. They'll be able to tell you what they've determined about the accusations the rehab place made against him." The officer tore a page from his notebook and handed it to Sam.

He glanced at it to see that the officer had written those names as well as the address of the police station, with instructions for finding parking. Sam looked at the man's name badge. "Thank you, Officer Jenkins."

When Sam saw Richard lying on the exam table, his heart fell into his stomach. His looked smaller and frailer than Sam had ever seen.

A gash at the hairline still trickled blood down the older man's forehead. The knot forming around the wound was already purpling. His left cheekbone appeared scraped and bloody. Vivid bruises colored his left shoulder and his forearms. There were more on his upper right arm, though they were yellow and green.

"Dad!"

"Where's my grandson?"

"Ethan's in jail. The people from Bayou say he attacked an attendant and pushed you down."

Richard tried to rear up on one arm before groaning and dropping flat.

"You go get my grandson! He was trying to help me. That attendant has been bullying residents for months. I tried to tell you. Ethan tried to tell you. But you were too busy to listen. Or maybe you didn't care. Whatever. Just go get my grandson. I want to see him."

Sam staggered backwards and fell onto a hard, metal chair sitting against the wall. He looked from the doctor to the police officer. Both wore expressions of sympathy. But Sam saw only secret condemnation for his failure to pay attention.

Officer Jenkins moved closer to Richard in the small room. "Let's continue with your statement if you feel up to it."

"As soon as my son gets out of here."

Sam didn't remember getting up and walking into the hallway. He finally became aware of the doctor standing next to him. The man's hand was on Sam's shoulder, and he was saying something Sam couldn't hear over the voice of guilt shouting in his head.

Finally, Doctor Bowen's words got through to Sam's racing brain. "He didn't mean it like that. He's been distraught. I understand that you've had a devastating shock. Unfortunately, elder abuse is more common than you think. Because Richard told Officer Jenkins what was going on as soon as they were alone, we have a valid reason to prevent the nursing home representatives from seeing him. You don't have to worry about them right now."

"Go get your son out of jail. By the time the two of you get back, we'll have completed all our tests on your father, and the police will have questions for you about Richard's care at the facility."

"Tell me first, what's the extent of Dad's injuries?"

"Some of that bruising you saw is old, so I'm not worried that he won't heal from that. He has a slight concussion, but that will mend with rest. I'm worried he may have reinjured one of the discs repaired in his surgery last month. That's why I want to call in his surgeon and run some scans. Your father is in good hands, I promise. And it will help him calm down if he knows Ethan is alright." The doctor kept pace with Sam as he moved toward the waiting room door.

"I'll hold you to that promise, Doctor. And I'll be back as soon as possible with Ethan. Please make sure my father understands that."

It was a good thing the Bayou representatives were gone when Sam walked through the swinging doors.

CHAPTER SEVENTEEN

UNLIKELY MVP

After Sam blurted out what he'd discovered, Mike insisted on driving. When they reached the police station, Sam went inside while Mike parked the SUV. He'd also volunteered to call a lawyer friend.

Sam told the desk sergeant who he needed to see. Within five minutes, an officer came through a secure door and escorted Sam down a corridor into the station. The plainclothes officer who opened the door of the small interview room stepped out of Sam's way, and he caught the first glimpse of his son.

Ethan sat on one side of a metal table, holding a blue icepack to his face with one hand, pointing at something on the screen of a laptop computer with the other. Another officer stood behind him, looking over the boy's shoulder.

"Ethan!"

"Dad!" Ethan jumped out of his chair and rushed into Sam's arms.

He hugged the boy so hard that Ethan pushed back. "Too tight. Gotta breathe."

Sam eased his grip but held on to the boy's shoulders. "Are you alright?" He examined his son for injuries. Ethan's right eye was a violent mix of red, purple, and black, and a small cut oozed on his upper lip.

"Who hurt you?"

"I'm okay. How's Grandpop? They wouldn't let me go to the hospital with him." Ethan's anxiety over his grandfather's well-being was plain on his face.

"Your grandfather has a concussion and lots of bruises. You're going to be a matched set with that black eye. But the doctor is taking excellent care of him. Grandpop wanted me to come and help you." Sam took a deep breath and drew Ethan down to sit beside him on one side of the table. "Son, your grandfather says the attendant hurt him. But the CEO of Bayou says you attacked the attendant and your grandfather."

Ethan scowled and drew away from his father. "So, you believe them instead of Grandpop or me?"

Sam took a deep breath, hoping with all his might that he would serve Ethan in this pivotal moment. "No, Son, I don't believe them. I know you, and I know your Grandpop. I will figure this out and make it right. Do you trust me?"

The boy searched his father's face while Sam waited.

"Yeah, I do." He threw himself back into Sam's arms and sobbed.

When Ethan had cried himself out, Sam looked around and discovered the officers had left the room to give father and son time to comfort each other. He didn't know what came next, but he was pulling together everything Mike had taught him. Today could be the most important At Bat of his life.

When the door opened, a plainclothes officer carrying a laptop stepped back into the room.

"Mr. Masterson, I'm Detective Frank Torres." He paused and indicated a second man who carried two cans of soda, which he offered to Sam and his son. "This is my partner, Jimmy Fleet."

Sam waited until Ethan popped the top of his soda and sipped. Then he turned to the detectives. "Please tell me about the charges against my son and what I have to do to get him released. Officer Jenkins is taking my father's statement about the incident at Bayou."

The detectives took seats on the other side of the table. Detective Torres opened a folder. "Yes, we have his report. The other two responding officers are writing their reports right now. Ethan helped us while we waited for you. We think he's given us the evidence we need."

"I don't understand. How would Ethan have evidence for you?" Sam was out of his depth. Did the detective mean Ethan had proven his account of what happened or that he'd talked himself into deeper trouble?

"What did you tell them, Ethan? You should have waited until I could get here."

"No, Dad. It's okay. They believe Grandpop and me. They have to 'cause I showed them proof."

"How and where did you get proof?"

Torres placed the laptop on the table. Sam had forgotten all about it until now. When he looked closer, it looked like Ethan's.

"Thanks for loaning us your laptop, Ethan. We got everything we need for a warrant."

"Against my son?" Sam surged to his feet, ready to do battle.

"Sorry." Torres held his hand up to signify no harm. "I should have worded that better. Let me tell you what your son has done."

Sam eased back into his chair, wary but willing to listen calmly.

"It seems Bayou hired a new IT guy about two months ago, and he wasn't too careful about some hidden cameras," Torres explained.

"Wait. What? There are cameras in the Bayou building? How did I not know that?"

"Yeah. Turns out management has hidden cameras in all the residents' rooms and public areas. If their clients don't know about them, the company is in violation of a Florida statute."

"And Ethan found out about this? How?"

Ethan's eyes lit up when he turned to his dad. "See, the IT guy created an open port in the facility firewall. When I was visiting Grandpop one day, I was trying to get on Wi-Fi and noticed it. That seemed weird, so I showed it to Grandpop. We decided to click on it and couldn't believe what we saw. There are hidden cameras in the patients' rooms!

"Earlier that week, Grandpop was telling me about this attendant, Pauly, pushing some of the patients around, harassing them because they didn't do what he wanted fast enough. That's when I got the idea that I could check on Grandpop through the camera in his room to make sure he was okay in case that Pauly guy ever did something to him. I asked Grandpop for his permission, and then I started recording the feed from his room just in case. A few days later the port closed, but I found a way around it so I could watch over Grandpop."

"You... wow, I don't know what to say." Sam looked at the detectives.

"Yeah, we were impressed too," Torres added. "No wonder the Air Force is interested in Ethan's computer skills."

"Say, what?" Sam looked at his son. "Since when does the Air Force even know about my son?"

We're a team, and he needs to know he has my support.

"No big deal. I competed in a code-writing contest they sponsored during the science fair. It was back in freshman year. The Air Force sent a guy to talk to me about aerospace engineering and ask me to consider their college programs when I'm ready. Mom and I had been talking about it. We were going to tell you. Honest! But then she..." Ethan stared at the tabletop.

Sam wanted to reach out and hug him but didn't know if Ethan would resent him doing that in front of the detectives. *To heck with that,* Sam thought. *My son needs a hug, and he's getting one right now. We're a team, and he needs to know he has my support.*

He pulled Ethan into his arms for a brief but heartfelt hug. He released his son with a kiss on top of his disheveled hair.

"Dad!" Ethan protested, but Sam could see his gesture had pleased his son.

"What does this mean for Ethan and my dad?" Sam returned to the business of getting his son back where he belonged.

"Ordinarily, we'd be talking to Ethan about the legality of hacking. But, since the information will be vital to bringing a case against the Bayou Rehabilitation Resident Center, I'm fairly sure Ethan will get off with a slap on the wrist and a caution."

Father and son each took a deep breath and sat back in their chairs.

Detective Fleet answered what his partner left out. "What your son showed us means we know what happened in the altercation. And it's not what the rehab people are saying. Here's a recording of the incident, for which you should thank the careless IT guy. Take a look." He typed a few letters onto the laptop and turned it so they could all see the screen.

On the screen was a corner of Richard's room at Bayou. Sam's dad was sitting in the straight-back chair his surgeon had stipulated for his recovery process. A tall, beefy guy dressed in the rehab center's uniform walked into view. He spoke to Richard, who reached out for his walker. Sam saw the attendant pull the walker out of reach while Richard stretched for it until he grimaced in pain. Then the attendant slammed it into Richard's shins and grabbed his arms, forcibly lifting him from the chair.

Richard got one hand on the walker and tried to move it in front of him, but one metal leg hit the attendant's hip. That's when the attendant slammed Richard into the nearby wall. Sam's father slid down the wall and crumpled on the floor. The vicious look on the attendant's face changed to enjoyment as he pushed Richard into the wall every time the man tried to pull himself up.

A second later, the watchers saw Ethan run into view and grab the attendant's arm. The guy casually shrugged Ethan off. When the boy came back at him, the attendant punched him in the face. He laughed and said something to the boy and his grandfather, who huddled together against the wall. The bully turned his back on his victims, then pulled his phone out and made a call. Seconds later, the room filled with security officers and other staff.

Detective Fleet reached over and stopped the video. No one spoke.

Sam was breathless with rage. A person entrusted with Richard's care had deliberately and maliciously hurt his father and his son, and then lied about it. He closed his eyes. He could hear the detectives moving around, closing the laptop, shuffling papers. All

Sam wanted to do was race from the room and find that attendant. He wanted to hurt the man.

His phone pinged.

Sam opened his eyes and looked at the text from Mike.

My attorney friend, Carl, is ready for your call. Hang in there. You're going to Win Some here.

How did Mike always know when Sam needed a boost? Instead of following his anger and racing off for vengeance, Sam placed his elbows on the table and rested his head in his hands. Ten deep breaths later, he felt ready to talk to the detectives again.

"Where do we go from here?"

Detective Fleet explained, "We get a warrant, coordinate with some other departments, and go after Bayou, the attendant, and management."

Sam leaned across the table. "I want to be there when you go in."

"Oh, believe me; you're going to take point, Sam." Detective Torres gave him a wolfish grin. "In the meantime, take your boy to see his grandfather. We'll get in touch when we're ready to move."

"How long will that be?"

"Before the end of the day."

"Good," said Ethan. He and Sam headed to the door.

"Wait." Detective Torres stepped closer to Ethan.

The boy looked at his father, anxious that the officers had changed their mind about allowing him to leave.

"You may not realize this, but you're a hero, Ethan. Few people your age would confront a bully as big as Pauly. And even fewer would have the skills you used to find the videos for us to use as evidence. There are a lot of people in the Bayou Center who will be safer because you did the right thing. Thank you."

The detective held out his hand. Ethan smiled and shook it, then shook hands with Detective Fleet.

Sam and Ethan were out the door when Torres said, "If you decide the Air Force isn't interesting enough, give me a call. We can always use someone with your computer skills and sharp mind."

Ethan's smile turned into a huge grin as Sam put his arm around his son's shoulder and walked out of the station to meet Mike.

CHAPTER EIGHTEEN

FOR THE WIN

Sam walked through the front door to the Bayou Rehabilitation Resident Center just past seven that evening, dressed for business and feeling in control. After talking with Mike's attorney friend, Carl English, Sam had a plan to lead with calm, professional confidence. He would not be shaken. Carl stood shoulder-to-shoulder with him. Behind them, Detectives Torres and Fleet stayed in the background.

Felicia Young was on her way out, head down, looking at the file folders she was stuffing into a huge designer handbag. She spoke in a terse undertone to Wendell Hambleton while she strode across the lobby two steps ahead of the attorney. When she looked up, her stride faltered as she took in Sam's suit and tie. A second later, she raised her chin and smirked.

"Gentlemen, visiting hours are over. You'll have to come back tomorrow." She stepped forward as if to go around them.

"Oh, but we're not here to visit, Felicia. May I call you Felicia?" Sam gave her his most winsome smile. "We're here to talk to management. I believe that would be you. Lucky for us, you're the first person we see when we arrive."

"And I'm on my way out."

"We'd appreciate it if you'd delay that, Ms. Young. I think it will be advantageous for both parties," Carl said smoothly. "I'm Carl English, Mr. Masterson's attorney."

Felicia looked Sam up and down. "Do you seriously think you can threaten to sue Bayou, and we'll drop the charges against your son?"

"Oh, I'm not going to threaten to sue, Felicia. That's already underway."

Carl interjected, "If you prefer to conduct this discussion in the lobby, we're quite comfortable with that. But I suggest we take this somewhere private." He looked around as if only then noticing several residents and staff within hearing distance. Sam got the feeling his new lawyer took no prisoners.

Felicia sneered, then turned to march down a nearby hallway. Hambleton followed in her wake like a cowed puppy. Once inside the large, elegant office, she moved behind the massive desk to establish dominance.

Carl ignored her, pulling out the chair at the head of a large conference table before placing his briefcase on the table. Sam took his cue and sat in the next chair. When the detectives walked into the room and took chairs on the other side of Carl, Felicia threw up her hands in frustration and joined them. The Bayou lawyer pulled out the chair next to his client but slid it several inches away from her. He pulled a notepad from his briefcase and lined it up on the edge of the table.

"If you insist on doing this now, let's get it over with. I have plans for my evening." She directed her gaze at Sam. "Do you really believe you can sue Bayou and win? Our parent company spans the continent, and we have hundreds of lawyers on the payroll. Do you want to guess how long we can drag this out before a case ever goes to trial?"

"Ms. Young, you should let me speak with Mr. Masterson's lawyer," Hambleton advised.

"Shut up, Wen. I don't need anyone to speak for me. I'll let you know when I'm ready for you to throw your legal terms around."

Wendell Hambleton pursed his lips and slapped his notepad closed. Sam glimpsed anger in the lawyer's eyes before the man folded his hands on top of the notepad and stared fixedly at a painting on the wall.

Felicia tapped one long, red fingernail on the table and turned to Sam. "As I've already stated, Mr. Masterson, your father was to blame for the incident. And your son escalated the situation with his own violent assault on our attendant and on his own grandfather. There's no question that Bayou Rehabilitation Resident Center is the victim here."

Sam was ready for her. "That doesn't explain how you and your staff allowed him to be injured while in your care."

She said, "It's possible that Mr. Masterson—Richard—sustained some bruises while being lifted onto the gurney."

Sam frowned and glanced at his lawyer before admitting, "I suppose that could happen if he were combative."

"Yes. As I explained earlier, your son attacked your father's attendant, Pauly Rottin—"

Sam couldn't help himself. He snickered. "Really? The guy's name is Rotten?"

The detectives glanced at each other, then looked away, trying to hide their amusement.

She sniffed, "It's spelled R-O-T-T-I-N. And I don't know what that has to do with this situation. As I was saying, your son assaulted Pauly and then turned on his grandfather. We were lucky Pauly was there to stop him from doing Richard greater harm. We have multiple witnesses who confirm those facts." Her smile couldn't have been more virtuous. "Now I suggest you reconsider where you spend your time and energy. You'd be better off getting that son of yours some help for his anger issues. Perhaps you can make it a joint father-and-son project." Felicia dared Sam to lose his temper.

Carl looked over the top of his glasses as he calmly laid his pen on top of the yellow legal pad on which he'd been taking notes.

"Do you know who Sam is, Ms. Young?"

For the first time, Felicia looked uncertain. "Of course I do. He's the son of Richard Masterson, who has been a resident patient here for just over a month."

"And who signs the checks for the very expensive care Richard Masterson supposedly receives at this facility?"

"Mr. Masterson. Sam Masterson. I don't see what that has to do with anything. It's not yet decided whether Richard will be allowed back into this facility. And I assure you, Bayou Rehabilitation Resident Center has an exceptionally long waitlist."

"I'm sure you're right. About the waitlist. You may even be right about having enough legal power to drag this out forever. But not about my client's ability to withstand a long, drawn-out court battle. Or about the certainty that during the trial, your name and that of your company will be in the headlines. Let me remind you that Sam has enough fans and friends to keep any case he's involved in front and center in the news cycle every day."

"So what? You threaten our company with bad publicity, and I'm supposed to drop the charges against his son?"

"See, that's where I don't need your help, Felicia. Let me introduce the two gentlemen across the table—the two you've been ignoring." Sam leaned toward her. "Meet Detectives Torres and Fleet. They have some information for you."

Each man gave her a casual wave as Sam said their names. She threw a confused look at them before turning back to Sam.

"What information?"

Detective Torres took the lead. "Well, first off, we're happy to tell you we have no intention of bringing charges against young Ethan Masterson. In fact, he may get a medal." He paused for her reaction.

"Impossible! I told you what happened here." For the first time, Felicia appeared concerned.

"So you have. But we've seen the videos taken by your hidden cameras."

The blood drained from her face. "I don't know what—"

"Tell it to the judge. And I'd fire your IT guy if I were you. We'd never have caught on if he'd been any good at his job." Torres stood and moved around the table toward the CEO of Bayou.

"Let's continue this conversation downtown. Mr. Masterson and his attorney have plans for this evening. Plans that don't include mugshots and fingerprints. I think we've delayed them long enough."

"But I can't leave this facility without anyone in control."

"Don't worry about your patients, Ms. Young. While we've been having this fascinating discussion, the state Agency for Health Care and Administration has been putting people in place to keep Bayou operating until someone honest and dependable can take over. They've also been notifying families about today's events. Oh, and we've arrested Pauly Rottin for assault and battery. I'm sure he'll have an interesting story for us about how this place runs."

The detective snapped cuffs around her wrists.

She turned to Wendell Hambleton. "Wen, you're my lawyer. Do something."

"I would, Felicia, if I had any legal terms to throw around. But since I represent Bayou Rehabilitation Resident Center, not you, I'm left with nothing to say to someone who appears to have abused their position and lied to the police except, 'see you in court.'"

He stood and walked out of the room.

Felicia's pretty face twisted with anger as she struggled against the cuffs. She spat at Sam, "I detest sports and the stupid jocks who play them."

When the police officers led her from the room, Sam felt like he could breathe again.

He turned to Carl. "I can't thank you enough for answering Mike's call and getting here so fast. I couldn't have done this without your help. If there's ever anything I can do for you, I'd be honored to be of service."

> "I recognized Mike's influence as soon as we met tonight. He worked a miracle in my life too."

"See, that right there is why I came. I recognized Mike's influence as soon as we met tonight. He worked a miracle in my life too." Carl clapped his hand on Sam's shoulder. "I enjoyed being on your Win Some team especially for something as important as stopping elder abuse. My parents are getting to the age where we may have to hire caregivers. It feels good to know we took at least a couple of bad players out of the game tonight.

"You were a great teammate, took your cues, and knocked this thing wide open. Your father will be proud of what you've done. Let's stay in touch, Sam."

"I'd like that. Now, let's get out of here so you can get home to your family."

The men shook hands and walked out together. Sam stopped in the parking lot to text Mike.

It's done. Couldn't have made it without your help. Thank you!

It was only a few seconds before Mike replied.

Hooray for the team. Heard you stayed Win Some.

Sam laughed and keyed his phone again.

I was so Win Some I gave Felicia Young cavities.

CHAPTER NINETEEN

PRACTICE PAYS OFF

The long day caught up with Sam while he rode the hospital elevator to Richard's room. Visiting hours were long over here as well, but the floor nurses knew Sam would be returning that night. Sam and Mike had used their Win Some skills to get the doctors and nurses on their team about that. Now, the nurse at the desk raised her head when she heard his quiet footsteps and gave him a brief smile before returning to her paperwork.

When Sam reached his father's room, he carefully eased the door open, not wanting to disturb Richard if he was sleeping. In the dim light, he saw his son sitting in a chair close to his grandfather's bed. The boy leaned forward, head resting on the blanket, close to Richard's right hand. He was fast asleep, as was Richard.

Movement from the corner of the room caught Sam's attention. He turned to see Mike rise from a second chair and motion to the hallway. Sam followed him out the door and pulled it closed behind them.

"Mike, I can't thank you enough for staying with Ethan and Dad until I could get back here."

"No thanks needed. I was happy to help. Now that you've sorted out Felicia Young and her abusive staff, what's next for the Masterson family?"

"The first thing on the agenda is Dad's recovery. The scans showed some bruising and swelling around the areas where he had surgery. His surgeon wants to monitor him for a couple of days. After that, Dad will have to start physical therapy all over again."

"And Ethan?"

"He's in the clear for now. He and Dad may be called to testify at a trial if the Bayou people let it go that far. Carl doesn't think they'll want the bad publicity. They won't want to risk losing their clients or their licenses because of a few bad actors. He thinks their board of directors will take action to remove Ms. Young from her position." Sam swiped his hand down his face, hard, feeling the enormity of the situation catch up with him. "I hope the abusers we stopped tonight were the only ones in that corporation. I have a feeling they're not, but there's no way to know."

"You've done a good thing in calling out those people's abuse of power." Mike replied. "This mess is going to spread fast and soon it will be common knowledge that Bayou had abusive staff. More people, more patients, may come forward with their stories. You did an even better thing in making it right for your family. They'll be proud of you." Mike placed his hand on Sam's shoulder for a moment. "And I'm proud of you for how well you employed your Win Some skills. It couldn't have been easy to stay focused and control your emotions after learning the truth about what took place at Bayou."

Sam gave Mike a half-smile, all he had the energy to summon. He caught sight of the clock at the desk. "Hey, it's tomorrow already, man. Or I guess a new today. You'd better get out of here so you can get some rest."

Mike glanced at his watch and nodded. "Let me know if I can help in any other way,."

"Hey, I know you probably did a lot of this because it's your job to take care of the players. But you went way beyond for us. I won't ever forget how you stepped up. It's like you were truly part of my team."

"I *am* part of your team. And you're part of mine. Don't you see that we're all part of a bigger team? That's what being Win Some is about. Being teammates, focusing on what everyone on that team needs until we all get the win. Until our world gets the win."

Sam yawned. "It's too late to talk tonight, but I want to hear how you got so Win Some in the first place. I have a feeling you have more lessons for me. And I'm ready to learn them. No, I *need* to learn them."

"I do have a couple more Win Some steps for you. But they can wait a few days while you get the Masterson family home and settled again. Do you mind if I pray for your father's recovery?"

Sam impulsively pulled his friend into a hug. Tears burned his eyes.

"You have my permission, and I'm sure Dad would give his if he were awake." He stopped and cocked his head to take a deeper look at the clubbie. "Somehow, I think any prayers from you go right to heaven's head office. Thanks again."

The friends nodded to one another and bumped fists. Then Mike turned to walk toward the elevator.

Sam slipped back into his dad's room. He quietly went to one knee at the side of the bed across from Ethan and placed his hand over his father's. The older man stirred and opened his eyes a slit.

> "That's what being Win Some is about. Being teammates, focusing on what everyone on that team needs until we all get the win."

"Sorry, Dad, I didn't want to wake you. I just needed to know you're all right."

"Hmph. Did you take care of those bullies at the rehab home?" Richard's eyes slid closed.

"Done and dusted. You would have been proud."

"Good boy." Richard squeezed Sam's hand.

Hearing his father's approval, Sam took a deep breath he hadn't been aware he needed. He felt lighter than he had in hours.

"Who was that guy who waited with us? I like him."

"His name is Mike. He's the clubbie for the Millers and most importantly, he's my friend."

"You need more friends like that. You know, he even prayed for my recovery. Nobody's prayed for me since your mother died."

"You pray? I had no idea."

"Well, how are you gonna get what you need if you don't ask? Now you'd better get this youngster home to bed. He's had a hard day. You should let him stay home from school tomorrow," Richard whispered.

"It's Saturday already. But I'll make sure he gets to sleep in. Then we'll be back to see you." Sam watched his father's face.

"Don't want you to get in trouble with the team for missing practice or a game."

"Not up for negotiation, Dad. If they don't understand why my place is with you right now, they'll just have to fire me."

Richard reached his other hand to touch Ethan's hair. "Wake up, boy."

Ethan jerked upright in surprise, looking immediately to see if his grandfather was okay. When he saw his dad, he stretched and yawned loudly. "Sorry, I didn't mean to fall asleep."

"It's time for the two of you to get out of here so this old man can get some sleep," Richard growled. He pulled at the sheet and thin blanket and closed his eyes. "Go on, get gone. I want some sleep before the nurses bring around all their equipment, and wake me up for more tests."

Ethan turned the top of the sheet down over the edge of the blanket. Watching him, Sam realized his son was recreating the way Aileen used to tuck Ethan into bed when he was much younger. "See you tomorrow, Grandpop."

"Yeah, I know you will. You're a good kid." A small smile teased at Richard's lips.

"Goodnight, Dad." Sam stood and started to release his father's hand. But the older man tightened his grip.

"Good boy," he murmured. Then he fell asleep.

Sam put his arm around Ethan's shoulder as they walked through the door and down the hall. They nodded to the nurse when they passed the desk.

"Thank you," he said and watched her smile bloom at his expression of gratitude.

Ethan pushed the elevator button and the doors opened. They stepped on board and Sam pushed the button for the main floor.

"Let's go home, Son."

CHAPTER TWENTY

A SACRIFICE FLY

"Are you sure you're all right with this, Ethan? It's going to mean a lot of changes around here for all of us." Sam wiped the sweat from his forehead before wrestling the dining room table onto its side so he could disassemble it.

Ethan stopped on his way out of the room with one of the upholstered chairs. "I'm sure, Dad. I think it's a great plan. Grandpop will get better a lot faster once he's here with us. And we'll get to see him every day." The boy swung the chair too close to the doorframe in his enthusiastic response. One sturdy wood leg struck the woodwork, denting it and knocking off a patch of paint.

"Sorry. I didn't mean to wreck the wall." Ethan put the chair down to inspect the damage.

"Those chairs are heavy, so you have to be a little more careful about how you hold them." Sam walked over to examine the doorframe. "That's not too bad. You should have seen the mess I made with a bookshelf I built in woodworking class. When I brought it home and tried to take it upstairs to my room, I didn't have it balanced and managed to knock a hole in the wall. Then when I jerked the corner of the shelf out of the hole, the other end swung around and hit the stair spindle so hard the spindle broke in half." He ran his fingers across the small dent.

"Wow, Grandpop must have been really mad. What did he do?"

"He took me to the woodshed."

"What? He whipped you?"

"No, he took me out there, told me to find a piece of drywall to fit the hole, and showed me how to patch the wall. Then he asked the woodworking teacher to show me how to make a replacement spindle."

Ethan smirked at his father. "I guess I'm going to learn how to fix this dent?"

"That you are. Let's get these last pieces moved out of here so the renovation team I hired can get in here tomorrow to turn the pantry into a new bathroom for your grandfather. Once we get this cleaned up, we'll take a quick trip to the store and get supplies for our repair job."

"I didn't know you knew how to do all this building and repair stuff. Did Grandpop teach you?" Ethan lifted one end of the tabletop and the two of them moved it into the family room. "Now that we've got all this furniture out of the dining room, what are we going to do with it? We can't leave it all in here, can we?"

Sam shook his head. "No, we have to get the floors in all the downstairs rooms clear so your grandfather can move around safely with his walker." He sat on the couch. "Let's take a break and figure this out."

Ethan threw himself down on the couch, sprawling across the cushions as if worn out. "Sure. Do you want some water? I'm thirsty. I'll get you some if you want it."

"Sounds like a plan. Thanks." Sam was surprised at Ethan's offer to do something for him. His boy was growing up. He didn't know how to begin their next conversation, so he took a minute to reflect on what he was going to ask Ethan to do and the best way to approach it. It was time to be Win Some again.

"Okay, here's the thing, Ethan. Grandpop isn't going to be able to climb the stairs here for a long time. That means we won't have a dining room."

"Yeah, I figured that." Ethan put his hands behind his head and leaned back into the cushions. "What does that have to do with getting all this stuff put somewhere else?"

"Well, we've kept everything the way it was when your mother was here. It made us both feel safer and more comfortable seeing her things every day. But having Grandpop living on the ground floor is going to be a big change. And we'll have to get used to having a home health aide living here. So, if we don't have a dining room, we really don't need dining room furniture."

Ethan sat upright. "But Mom chose everything in that room. I remember she spent two weeks deciding on the fabric for the chair seats." He got up and turned one of the dining chairs around so he could sit on it, facing his father. "We can't just forget that."

"No, we'll never forget your mother. We'll never forget all the things she did for us. But we must be real about what our new life without her looks like."

His son kicked at the floor with the toe of his tennis shoe, his eyes avoiding Sam's. "So, what are you saying? We're just going to throw away everything Mom liked?"

"That's not what I'm saying at all. In fact, I think we should each choose some of our favorite things that she brought into this house when she was making it into a home for us. We can keep those things forever. But I know your mom didn't care about things. She cared about the people she loved. And Grandpop was on that list. I think she would have been the first to say that we should bring him home and make his space as comfortable as we can."

Sam watched Ethan lean his elbows on his knees while he thought about that. He was trying hard to use the Win Some tools he'd learned so that he and Ethan could work together. This was new territory for both of them.

"So, what do you think we should do?"

"Why don't we think about what Mom would do if she were here? Then we can make plans that will let each of us get what we need."

"I don't know. That sounds awful smart. Are you feeling okay?" Ethan laughed and threw himself back onto the couch. Then he sobered. "I miss Mom. It's not the same without her."

> "Your mom didn't care about things. She cared about the people she loved."

"I miss her too, Son. Every minute of every day. But I think we know what she would say. She taught us well while she was with us." Sam tugged Ethan into an embrace and breathed a sigh of relief when his son rested his head on his shoulder.

Ethan pushed himself out of his father's arms. "I think I know what I want to keep. But do I have to make my decision right now?"

"No, take all the time you need. Do you want any of this dining room stuff?"

"Nope. What would I do with a dining room set? I'm just a kid. I like to eat on the couch," Ethan teased.

"Well, then what do you think Mom would do with furniture she didn't need?" Sam wanted his son to choose.

His son cocked his head, just like Aileen used to do, while he considered. "I think she would give all this stuff to the Habitat ReStore. That way, someone who needs it could have a nice table and the Habitat people could make some money to build more houses."

"Are you sure that's what you want?"

The boy nodded decisively. "That's exactly what I want." He turned to his father. "Hey, can I make the call for them to come pick the stuff up? That way, it will be like I'm helping share what she gave to us."

Sam had to clear his throat before he could answer. "I think that will be perfect. Your mom would be very proud of you. I know I sure am."

"Cool! Let's go to the hardware store and you can show me all the repair skills Grandpop taught you."

"Son, if you think that bookshelf accident was my one and only, you're going to have to start a list. I'm sure Grandpop will be happy to detail all my misadventures once we bring him home. But your little dent is an easy place to start." Sam stood and stretched. "Let's get the supplies and grab some lunch. We are going to be busy since there are only a couple of days to get everything ready. Would you like to pick out the best color for the walls?"

CHAPTER TWENTY-ONE

THE SWEET SPOT

Ethan worked with Sam during the entire weekend to get the dining room repainted before he brought Richard home. Sam felt closer to his son than he had for ages.

Now, as Sam watched his dad look around the renovated space, he could tell his father approved.

A recliner and two comfy chairs created a sitting area in the former dining room. One straightback chair stood in the middle of them. His father needed a hospital bed until he was strong enough to get himself in and out of bed. They'd placed it at one end of the room, near the exercise equipment Richard's doctor recommended. The home health aide had suggested they add a nightstand beside the bed. Sam had brought down the one that stood on Aileen's side of the bed.

"I don't want to put you to any trouble, Sammy. This looks like it will do." Richard sat in a wheelchair and waited until Chris Aguilar, his new aide, moved past him and turned down the covers on the bed.

"Hey, I've been spending too much time in bed lately. How about you help me into my recliner and let me adjust to my new home for a while?" Richard rolled his way toward the seating area.

"Sure, Mr. Masterson. But you're going to have to sit in the straight chair until we can get your back and abs strong enough to lift yourself out of a cushy recliner."

"Well, I'm sure not ready to lie down. I'm too old for naps. Don't forget that." Richard changed course and positioned himself in front of the straight-backed chair with arms. Sam knew better than to offer his help. But Chris moved right in. After locking the wheels, he helped Richard stand and ease himself onto the chair.

"I'm not decrepit yet, young man. I've been sitting myself down for longer than you've been on this green earth."

Chris only smiled. "I'm sure you're right. But since your son is paying me big bucks to help you get from here to there and to build muscles, would you do me a personal favor and let me do that? I don't want to lose this job because I have nothing to do all day but watch TV and eat bonbons."

His patient snorted. "Seems like a lot of fuss to me. And if there's anyone eating bonbons around here, it better be me."

"How about if I go get us some lunch?" Chris replied. "I can tell you're going to be one of my favorite patients, so I'm going to let you call me Chris."

"You're going to let me, huh? This old man can't get any respect these days. Okay, Chris, see what's on the menu today. I'm ready for some real food." Richard gave the young man a crooked grin and waved him away.

Once they were alone, Sam sat down to keep his father company.

"Looks like you did a lot of extra work to bring me home with you." Richard didn't look at Sam as he spoke.

"Ethan helped a lot. He did a lot of the painting, so be sure to let him know you like it, even if you don't."

Richard frowned. "What makes you think I don't like it?" He looked around again, noticing the newspaper on the end table next to his chair, copies of his favorite books on a shelf nearby, and the floor clear of rugs. He nodded toward the door leading into the new bathroom. "I don't remember that door being so wide."

"That's your bathroom. We figured you'd want some privacy. We also tried to make this place feel familiar and comfortable." Sam stared at his father. "I'm truly sorry the rehab home I found for you turned out to be so awful. And I apologize for believing I was too busy to hear what you needed to tell me. I just want you to know I'm working on myself and trying to do better."

"Well, you've made a good start on making up for it by getting me away from that snake pit of a rehab home." Richard slapped the arm of his chair.

Sam knew there wouldn't be a better time than now to start changing his relationship with his father.

"You're right to be disappointed with me. But from now on, we must be on the same team so we can bring this family back together the way Mom and Aileen would want us to be."

Richard just sat staring at the floor. "How do you plan on doing that?" Richard's tone sounded doubtful.

Sam grinned. "I'm going to be the most Win Some guy you've ever seen."

That got a look from his father. "You? Winsome? Aren't you a mite too old and bulky to be winsome? Next thing you'll be telling me you're going to skip around the house, tossing flower petals in front of my wheelchair everywhere I go."

Sam had to laugh at that image. "I'm sure you're picturing me in a tutu and ballet shoes. No, I'm not talking about being charming or childlike. This is a different Win Some, where I focus on serving instead of winning."

Richard looked at his son as if he didn't recognize him. "Serve what? Serve lunch?" When Sam didn't rise to his bait, he offered, "Okay. I give. Where's this change of attitude coming from? I can't describe our past relationship as all sunshine and lollipops, especially over the last year. But you do look and sound different today. Did that thing with that rotten fellow scare you? Let me tell you right now, I'm not planning on dying anytime soon. You don't have to be charming on my account." He turned his attention to the blank screen on the large television mounted midway along the long wall opposite the seating area and the bed.

> "This is a different Win Some, where I focus on serving instead of winning."

"It's not for your benefit. Well, it is in a way, because if I'm Win Some, we'll both be happier. It's about being aware that we're a family. And family is a team."

"Go Team Masterson!" Richard snarked.

Sam just smiled. Thinking about how he could serve his team got easier each time he used what Mike had taught him. Before this, he would have answered his father's questions with anger, believing Richard didn't approve of him. Now he saw them as opportunities to discover what his father needed. Sam was well acquainted with his father's reluctance to reveal anything personal. He'd always felt he had to try harder to win his father's approval because he had never been sure what his dad expected of him. Mike's example had shown him a new way to connect.

> "If I'm Win Some, we'll both be happier."

Sam reached across the short space between their chairs and grasped his father's hand like he'd done the night in the hospital. "You're important to Ethan and me, Dad. We love you. We want you with us for a very long time. I know we don't talk about things that matter, at least not often enough. But I'd like us to at least try. That's the only way I can make sure you get what you need out of our team effort."

Richard dipped his head to swipe at his eyes with his free hand. His fingers tightened on Sam's. When he finally spoke, his voice was gruff with emotion. "I may have been a little rough on you when you had too many things on your mind. I could have insisted that you stop and listen to what I wanted to say about that bunch of yahoos at Bayou." He sniffed, but continued, "You know I'm not much for words, but if you're willing to be patient with me, I'll do my best."

He raised his head and met Sam's eyes. "And let's get one thing clear right now. I'm proud of you, Samuel Isaiah Masterson. I always have been. You and Ethan are everything to me. So, I won't doubt my place in this family if you promise to never forget I have your back no matter what."

It was Sam's turn to brush tears away. "It's a promise."

They heard footsteps approaching down the hall. Richard took advantage of the distraction to ask, "Where did you get this Win Some idea?"

"A friend has been helping me. You met him at the hospital."

"The guy who found the lawyer for you and then stayed with Ethan and me?"

"Yeah, Mike Gilchrist. I told you about him that night, but you might not remember. It was late and you'd had a horrible day. Mike is the Millers' team clubbie. I think you'll like him a lot."

Richard patted Sam's hand and sat back in his chair. "I think you're right. I look forward to seeing him again. Tell him to come see me whenever he wants. I bet he can tell me some embarrassing stories about you."

Chris opened the kitchen door and asked, "Are you ready for this feast? I promise there's nothing remotely resembling hospital food here." He pushed a cart loaded with sandwiches and drinks into the room.

Richard looked over his plate. "Not bad, young fellow."

"Chris," the aide reminded him.

"Okay, tell me, Chris, what do you think about wearing a tutu while sprinkling flower petals in my path as I roll around the house?"

The young man didn't hesitate, giving a completely straight-faced answer, "Well, sir, my army ranger buddies didn't nickname me Twinkle-Toes for nothing. Good thing I packed my gold-sequined tutu and tiara. I presume you will provide the petals?"

Richard leaned back and laughed until he coughed. "We're gonna have to keep this one, Sam."

Once he caught his breath, he turned to Chris, "If you're going to twinkle those toes around me, you'd better call me Richard. And when we're done with lunch, you can help me into bed for a little shut eye."

Sam could tell his father was tiring but didn't want to remind him he'd said he was too old for naps. The look on his face must have given him away.

"I'm old enough I can change my mind whenever I please. Today I am pleased to rest so I can be fresh when my grandson gets home. He promised to show me the game he's designing on his computer. It boggles the mind. Why, when I was a kid, games were something we played outside with sticks and cans, or on boards when we came inside after dark. The world is sure different."

Chris and Richard fell into an easy conversation about the changes Richard had witnessed over the years. As Sam watched them chat, he realized this was the most comfortable he'd been with his father for years. It seemed like a miracle that he'd been able to have a positive conversation and clear some of the long-standing tension between them. He could hardly wait to tell Mike.

CHAPTER TWENTY-TWO

RUNS BATTED IN

It was the end of the week before Sam found an opportunity to sit down with Mike. They met early one morning at a small park near the stadium just before sunrise. Without discussing it, they gravitated toward a picnic table and took seats facing the sunrise.

Mike laughed when Sam described Ethan's reaction to the hundreds of paint color swatches they'd found at the hardware store. And his eyes sparked with approval when hearing about Sam's conversation with Richard. "You keep working ahead of my lessons. A few weeks ago it would have been hard for you to imagine having a heart-to-heart conversation with your father. But you trusted the process and trusted yourself to let your father see who you're working to become. Because you did, you slid right from step three, your At-Bat stance, into step four."

"Really? What is step four?" Sam couldn't hide his eagerness to move deeper into the Win Some methods.

"Okay. We're taking it back to the ball field again. So far, you've grabbed your bat, warmed up in the on-deck circle, and stepped up at bat, assessing the situation and choosing your swing. Now that you're there, what's your mission?"

"Bringing the runners home."

"Yep. Got it in one. You're not there to showboat and make history for yourself."

Sam grinned. "You mean I'm going to have to clear the bases in my relationships?"

"It's up to you to get the runs batted in. That is step four: Drive Runs Batted In, which is really about putting aside any selfish ambition and focusing on what your team needs in order to win. You may want a big hit every time you step up to the plate. Those hits are good for your stats, and they make you look like a superstar. However, sometimes the coach tells you to bunt because it's better for the team's strategy. When you are working for something bigger than yourself, you're willing to do whatever it takes for the team to win, right?"

> "Win Some works in every relationship. When you take the focus off yourself and think about others more, life works better. Everybody wins."

Sam scratched the back of his neck. "There must be more to it than letting all my teammates win. How does that help me get what I need out of the game?" He made air quotes around the word *game*.

"Think about it. We're talking in baseball terms because that makes it easy to remember the steps. But what's really at stake here? Always getting what you want or building healthy, fulfilling relationships with other people?"

"Yeah, I see what you're saying. I think we're getting into the part where I strike out the most."

"You don't have to strike out at all. You're letting this play with your brain. You've already proved you can master the concepts: Grab Your Bat, step into the On-Deck Circle, and take your At Bat. Runs Batted In is the result of learning and applying those processes."

"Are you sure I'm ready for this step?"

Sam's friend guffawed. "Man, you already got your first RBI. Look at where you are with Ethan and your dad. Do you really think you'd be talking to either of them like you have this past week if you hadn't applied everything I taught you?"

A slow dawning glow lit Sam's face. "I hadn't thought of it that way. In the past, I would have made a plan for my family and just forced Ethan and my dad to comply with it. No wonder we were always fighting. It was my way or the highway at all times." He nudged Mike in the ribs. "You gotta go slow for this rookie, buddy. Tell me how I make Win Some step four a grand slam."

"You have the skill and talent to do so many great things with your life. In the business world, you'll hear the term *servant leadership*. Those business leaders are using the same Win Some principles you are learning today. Win Some works in every relationship. When you take the focus off yourself and think about others more, life works better. Everybody wins."

"You know that's what I want," Sam insisted. "You've seen how hard I'm trying to make a difference for myself and everyone around me."

Mike nodded. "Your head and heart are in the right place. They weren't always working together in the past. But you're on the way now."

"But how will I know when I'm doing Win Some right? I still get into arguments with Ethan and my dad even when I'm practicing the steps you've given me. And there are times when I want to do things my way, when it feels like life would be so much easier if I wasn't supposed to make sure everyone gets what they want."

"Have you ever heard the expression 'Rome wasn't built in a day'?" Mike asked.

"Sure. But what if I do all the steps right and still don't bat any runners in? What if I think I'm building good relationships, but I'm only fooling myself about what everyone needs?"

"Well, I'd say you start with what *you* need. You have to know yourself so you can be authentic enough to build trust with other people. What do you want out of your relationships? Not just with your family and friends, but with everyone you meet?"

> "You have to know yourself so you can be authentic enough to build trust with other people."

Sam stared out over the ocean, thinking hard. "That's not easy to answer. I guess I never really sat down to think about what I need in a relationship. I've just gone where life leads me. You know, if someone was nice to me, I'd be

> "A Win Some person leads each encounter in the best direction because they're mentally prepared to love and serve."

nice back. But if they were rude or angry, my mood would reflect theirs. There have been a lot of ups and downs that way. I'd wait to see how the other guy was going to act before deciding how I would react."

"Life shouldn't be about reacting to whatever stress or tension someone else is carrying around. A Win Some person leads each encounter in the best direction because they're mentally prepared to love and serve. However, you can't lead anyone else if you don't know where you are going. What do you really want out of life?"

"Out of my life? Now it sounds like I'm supposed to have a five-year plan or something. I barely know what I'm doing from day to day."

Mike stood as the sun rose in front of them, throwing dazzling golden beams through the tree leaves. "Beautiful morning, Sam. It's a beautiful moment when we all have time to contemplate the coming day. You, my friend, need time to reflect. I'll leave you to it." He raised an eyebrow, nodded to Sam, and walked toward the parking area.

CHAPTER TWENTY-THREE

PURPOSE AND INTENT

Got the answer to your question. You free to talk today?

Sam hit send on the text to Mike.

He slammed his locker door shut as he prepared to hit the batting cage with Anker. The rookie was showing great improvement. Not only had he become a friend, but Sam had realized he liked sharing his knowledge with the newer players. He was glad the boss had chosen him to mentor the younger man.

Hugh Sutton had been silent since their chat following the video incident. Sam hoped that meant he was pleased with how he'd shaped up and with the work he was doing with Anker.

Two steps from the end of the tunnel, Sam's phone chimed to indicate an incoming text. He stopped to pull it from his pocket.

Looking forward to hearing your news. Have plans this evening. How about right after you win this afternoon's game? I'll meet you at the coffee shop.

Sam grinned at the clubbie's confidence in the team and keyed in his reply. Whistling "Holding Out for a Hero," an old Bonnie Tyler song he'd heard his dad play on the stereo hundreds of times when he was a little kid, Sam strode onto the field, intent on making this day Win Some in every way.

* * *

Iced coffee in hand, Sam joined Mike at a table near the back wall of the busy coffee shop.

"Congratulations on today's win." Mike raised his cup.

"Thanks for believing we'd win before we even hit the field." Sam returned his salute.

"Always."

"I know you have plans, and I don't want to hold you up, but I did want to tell you what I figured out."

Mike glanced at his watch. "We've got about forty minutes before I need to get on the road. But I do want to hear what you've discovered."

Sam suddenly looked down, avoiding his friend's eyes. He opened his mouth and closed it again. Mike waited patiently.

"You're going to think I'm crazy," Sam cautioned.

"Why don't you try me?" Mike sat back in his chair.

"Okay, here it is. I fell asleep while trying to figure out what I wanted. Everything I was coming up with felt trite and useless."

"*Useless.* Unusual word choice for such a simple question." Mike raised his cup to his lips, sipped, then returned it to the table-top, where he turned it in circles while observing Sam.

"Yeah, maybe not exactly what I'm trying to say. I mean, things like health, wealth, world peace. Isn't that what we all say? It's so glib and easy to pull that type of thing out of the air when someone asks what we want. I mean, it feels like I should want more than those pat answers."

"I agree."

Sam straightened his shoulders, took a deep breath, and said, "I saw Aileen last night."

"Your late wife," Mike clarified, watching Sam meet his eyes.

"Not like she was there in person or like a ghost. I dream about her a lot. But last night, she was sitting on the side of the bed watching me." Sam raised his hand. "Mike, I swear I felt the side of the bed dip. She put her hand over mine and I heard her say, 'Sam, you're making a mountain out of a molehill, as usual.' She tapped her finger over my heart to remind me of how she used to tease me. Then she said, 'Sweetheart, what have you done with purpose and intent?'" Sam paused to breathe. "Then I woke up, and she was gone. When I looked at the clock it was only 3:30 a.m., but I knew I wouldn't be sleeping any more."

"That's incredible." Mike leaned forward. "So, what answers did you find in the deep, dark hours before daybreak?"

"I realized I've gone my entire life making the easy choices. Or making decisions I thought would be to my benefit. In most cases, I did the things that would make the most money or fame, I'm afraid. I put myself and my career first. The only purpose-driven choice I ever made was marrying Aileen. I wanted to build a life and a family with her." Sam glanced up at Mike.

"I'm sorry your time together was so short."

"Thanks." Sam collected his thoughts again. "Anyway, I figured out why I never felt I could stop straining and reaching for something I couldn't even identify, something out of my reach. And Aileen's message made it clear for the first time. I never had real purpose. I never even thought about it. Life was all about me. You used the term *selfish ambition* the other day. That's what drove me."

> "From now on, my life is going to be about coming alongside people to help them win. I can't be all things to all people, but I can listen and help them reach as far as they can."

Mike nodded his understanding. "I hear you. So, tell me, what did you decide to do about that?"

Sam's smile reflected a new, calmer maturity. "I know my purpose. It felt great to help Anker improve his performance. I thought it would be a hassle, but I really enjoyed mentoring him. From now on, my life is going to be about coming alongside people to help them win. I can't be all things to all people, but I can listen and help them reach as far as they can."

He scuffed his hand over his hair. "Does that make sense, or am I completely missing what Aileen meant for me to discover?"

Mike looked the young ballplayer straight in the eye. "I think maybe for the first time in your life, you're choosing a direction rather than letting life push you around with the current."

Sam smiled. "Yeah, well, it's all new, and I'm not sure what it totally means yet. But as soon as I decided to live with purpose, it was like I felt Aileen's hand on my heart again. She was the smartest person I ever knew. She always knew the right thing to do not because she would get something out of it. Not to gain fame or fortune. But because she loved people and wanted to help."

"She sounds like a remarkable woman. I'm sorry I only met her a few times in passing." Mike set his empty cup on the table.

"Hey, I know you have plans for tonight. Thanks again for letting me get this off my chest. Like I said, I don't know where my purpose is leading me, but I'm open to discovering opportunities to serve." Sam glanced at his watch. "Do you have far to go? Will you get there in time?"

Mike leaned across the table to shake Sam's hand. "My men's study group is meeting just up the highway. I'll get there in plenty of time. Thank you for trusting me with your revelation. And I do want to talk about this in more depth. Now I'm sure you're ready for step five of the Win Some framework. How about we meet at the picnic table tomorrow morning?"

Sam held onto Mike's hand for a moment. "I'd like that."

After Mike walked out of the coffee shop, Sam sat there thinking for several minutes. He wondered what life would be like when he started using his new purpose to serve others. He didn't have any answers yet, but he felt hopeful. All of a sudden, he grinned and made his way out to the parking lot. He had a mission of his own. And this was the perfect time to accomplish it.

CHAPTER TWENTY-FOUR

CLEANING UP

Darla walked into the store manager's office and came to an abrupt halt when she saw Sam standing next to her boss. Confusion, fear, and resentment flickered across her face before she turned to the manager. "Avery said you wanted to see me, Mr. Grossman."

"I apologize, Darla, I asked Mr. Grossman to call you off the floor so I could talk with you," Sam said. "I know the last time I was here, I caused you hurt and embarrassment. That was cruel and thoughtless of me. Would you sit down for a few minutes and let me apologize?"

She looked from one man to the other, trying to read their intentions. When Sam waited patiently for her to decide, Mr. Grossman smiled and gestured to a chair in front of his desk. "You should hear Mr. Masterson out, Darla. He gave me his word that he doesn't intend to get you in trouble. I'll be right outside this door if you need me."

Again, she searched their faces. Mr. Grossman had always been fair, so she finally nodded and took a seat.

"Thank you." Sam waited until her boss exited the room and closed the door. He moved a second chair near hers and took a seat, so he wouldn't tower over her while they talked.

"I am terribly sorry for the way I talked to you. You did not deserve that at all. What happened was entirely on me. Please forgive me. I chose to work in a field where my life is more public than

119

most, and it's my responsibility to be gracious when people recognize me and want to share their excitement. What I did that night really made me look at myself and my attitudes. I can tell you that I've spent the time since then making decisions about the kind of person I want to be from now on."

Sam watched her eyes move around the room, pausing anywhere except on him. She knotted her hands in her lap. This conversation was harder than he expected. He took a deep breath and reminded himself to regrip. Darla seemed nervous. Time to build trust.

Sam smiled then continued, "I'm speaking from my heart. I'm truly sorry that I hurt you. This isn't me doing something to make myself look better in the eyes of the public. If you want me to make this apology in public, I'll do that. If you want to keep it between us, that's up to you too. But I want you to know I'm sincere about making this right with you."

> "I've spent the time since then making decisions about the kind of person I want to be from now on."

Darla raised her head to reveal teary eyes. "Well, if we're being honest, I'm partly to blame, Mr. Masterson."

"Sam."

"Well, Sam, then. I shouldn't have gone all fangirl on you when I could tell you were having a bad day. And I embarrassed your poor son. When I told my husband about it, he reminded me that you're just a man trying to get through life like the rest of us. Why, you were even doing your own grocery shopping. When I stopped to think about that, I mean, that surprised me, because you know, famous people have servants and cooks and all those people taking care of everything for them. But there you were getting canned chili and arguing with your son, just like I do some days.

"Then I felt terrible about the whole thing, but it was too late. All those people in the store that night had already uploaded all their videos." She shook her head.

"So, if you're man enough to come back here and offer an apology, then I can be woman enough to return the gesture." She stood up and held her hand out. "Mr. Masterson, Sam, I'm sorry too for my part in what happened that day. If we accept each other's apologies, does that mean we're square?"

Sam stood and gently shook her hand. "Darla, we are most definitely square." He grinned at her, "So, a son, huh? How old is he?"

Darla returned his smile. "Benny's eleven going on forty. Some days I think he's the greatest kid on earth. Others, I just want to shake some sense into him."

Motioning her back to her chair, Sam raised a finger in question. "Does Benny like baseball and hotdogs?"

"Of course he does. We live near the stadium, and my husband, Tom, takes him to the evening games when he's not too tired after getting home and when we can afford tickets."

> "If you're man enough to come back here and offer an apology, then I can be woman enough to return the gesture."

"Well, I'd like to invite you to a cookout the day after spring training ends. I've invited all the players and their families to my home. I'd be honored if you and your family would join us."

Her mouth fell open. "Are you sure? I mean, I made a mess out of your simple shopping trip."

"I'm positive. And we've agreed that's in the past. I hope we're friends now. Come out to my place. You'll have fun. There will be some burnt dogs and burgers." Sam wheedled with a grin.

Darla laughed. "Well, if we're talking burnt offerings, I accept for the three of us."

"Great, give me your email and I'll send the official invitation along with an address." Darla pulled a sticky note from the pad on her boss's desk and started writing. They stood at the same time, and she handed Sam the paper.

"So, do you want me to tell Mr. Grossman that I'll be going out to the cashier lane to make a public apology? I've sworn him to secrecy no matter what you choose."

"No. You coming to see me in private made me believe you meant it. Can I tell my husband that we're friends now?"

"Tell anyone you want. I'm proud to have a friend like you." Sam looked her in the eyes and smiled.

Darla leaned forward and gave him a quick hug. "Bye, friend. See you at your cookout. I can't wait to tell Benny and Tom." She opened the door and said, "Thanks for this, Mr. Grossman. We're all good here." She walked away with a spring in her step.

*　*　*

Two hours later, Ethan shouted down the stairs at Sam, who was getting ice cream for his dad and himself. "Hey, Dad, did you ever go back to the grocery store after that video came out?"

Sam walked out of the kitchen and looked at his son, standing at the top of the stairs with his phone in hand. "Why?"

"So did you?"

"As it happens, I was there this evening. Do you want some of the ice cream?" Sam lifted a heaping bowl before he turned to walk into Richard's room. Behind him, he heard the thunder of his teenager racing downstairs.

"First, you got ice cream and didn't tell me? And second, have you seen the video that lady you yelled at posted tonight?"

Sam felt a shiver of disquiet but told himself Darla wouldn't stab him in the back. *Would she?* "First, if you want ice cream, you know where it is. Second, I know nothing about any video."

Ethan smirked and handed his phone to his father before hurrying to the kitchen. "Do we have any chocolate chips to go on top?" he hollered.

"You also know where we keep those."

Richard spoke up, "Tell him if he finds those chips, I want some too. Why didn't you offer me toppings? I don't rate?" He wriggled his eyebrows to let Sam know he was teasing.

Sam placed his own bowl on the TV tray in front of his father. "Let me look and see what Ethan's talking about. I thought Darla and I straightened everything out."

Sure enough, it was Darla's face in the video paused on the screen. He pressed play.

"So, I just wanted you to know that video y'all were watching and talking about a couple weeks ago isn't the real Sam Masterson. Oh sure, that was him in the store that day. But I got a chance to meet the guy when he's not having a bad day. He's polite, he's funny, and he's not all thinking he's too good for everyone else.

"For all y'all out there who said he's a rich jerk playing on his fame, that's not true. He didn't have to apologize 'cause I kind of caused what happened. But he did—and straight to my face. He didn't get on TV or make some video of his own saying none of it was his fault; he just let all y'all call him names. And he didn't bring cameras when he came to make things right with me. He coulda done that so everyone would see what a big man he was, and how magnanimous he was to a poor little grocery clerk. But he didn't do that either.

"Sam Masterson is a decent man who had a bad day. So y'all just get over this and get yourself out to the stadium and support the teams that bring all their money to our town." She paused, then added, "Oh, and I don't think anyone would be mad if y'all did some shopping at our store. You never know. You might run into some really nice, reeaally fiiiiine ball players there."

Darla winked at the camera as she drawled out the last few words and the video ended.

"Wow, I did not see that coming," Sam admitted.

Richard lifted the last spoonful of ice cream to his lips. He swallowed and said, "She sounded like a pretty decent person herself."

"You'll get to see for yourself. I asked her and her family to the cookout."

Richard grunted and set his empty bowl on the tray table. "You better be hoping her husband isn't some huge jealous bruiser after the way she said you were so fine." He made quote marks around the word in question.

"I don't believe she mentioned my name. It was more about all ball players being fine specimens." Sam reached for the bowl he'd abandoned to watch the video but found only two empty bowls. He stared at his dad in amazement. "Tell me you didn't just eat your ice cream and mine while I was distracted."

"You snooze, you lose, Sonny." This time, Richard chortled until Ethan drifted back into the room with a heaping bowl of ice cream covered by a mound of chocolate chips.

Sam plucked it from his hands. "Thank you, Son." He dug his spoon in and closed his lips over the creamy mouthful.

It was Ethan's turn for indignation. "What happened to yours?"

"Your grandfather."

The boy nodded. "Gotcha. This time I'm taking my dessert straight to my room." He made it as far as the door before throwing over his shoulder, "At least I'll be growing taller with every mouthful, while you guys will grow..." He made a big stomach motion in front of his skinny frame.

Two voices in unison ordered, "Get outta here, kid."

CHAPTER TWENTY-FIVE

THE BATTING CAGE

It promised to be another hot, bright day. The barest tip of the sun edged the horizon, turning the bottoms of the high clouds rosy while gilding the tops of the waves meeting the park's shore.

"This is becoming our regular meeting place," Sam said as he and Mike took seats at the picnic table.

Mike replied, "I like to start my day here with the ocean and sky changing color to remind me how I've changed, and that each day is a new opportunity to leverage that into something positive and beautiful."

"If you don't mind me asking, how did you need to change? You're the calmest, most together person I've ever met." Sam turned to look at his friend.

"I wasn't always this way. When I was younger, I had a temper that I often allowed to get out of hand. I was impatient and selfish. That young man was sure he had all the answers. But he found out how wrong he was."

"I can't picture you that way. How did you leave that person behind and become the man you are today? The mentor you are to me?" Sam's attention shifted from the changing light to focus on his friend.

Mike laughed. "Don't think it was easy. I had to live through the consequences of some wrong choices and learn extremely painful lessons on the way."

"I'm sorry. I shouldn't have pried."

"No, you're fine. And my story is a good example for your fifth Win Some lesson."

"Yeah? Where do we start?" Sam asked.

"How about at the beginning? I told you I learned some painful lessons to get where I am now. Well, one of those was that you never arrive at your goal because there's always room for improvement." Mike's eyes were on the rising sun.

"What kind of improvement?"

> "Once you see the evidence, you can evaluate what worked, diagnose where you need to change, and then adjust your practice to improve."

"Let me tell you about the young man who was angry and never satisfied. He wanted to play baseball but wasn't good enough. He wanted to be rich and famous, but no one where he came from ever made anything of themselves. He set out to get what he thought he deserved no matter what it took. The way he chose to do that was with a gun."

Sam looked at his friend in disbelief. "This can't be your story. That's not the man I know."

"No. It's not. That man doesn't exist anymore. But he made his play one day and was so bad at robbing a store that he did it when an off duty cop was there. Long story short, the law stopped the angry young man before he made a bigger mistake. The judge offered him a choice, serving time or serving his country. He thought the military would be a breeze." Mike laughed and shook his head.

"Off the young man went to Afghanistan, where he learned there were things far worse than the life he hated so much. And where he made friends and lost them. And lost a piece of himself—body and soul."

Mike tugged up his left pant leg to reveal a prosthetic foot. Sam had always noticed a slight hitch in Mike's step and that he never wore shorts. Now it all made sense.

"Mike, I had no idea. I'm really sorry."

"Don't be. Losing part of my leg was the tipping point that made me realize my life was going nowhere. Luckily, it was at Walter

Reed that I first found out about living a Win Some life. That made me stop to consider where I was, how I got there, and what I had to do to turn my life around. It's been a learning and practicing process ever since."

"Wow. I don't know what to say." Sam turned his gaze back to the small waves breaking on the shore. "What did you do? I mean, I think I would have been so angry with life that I would have made everything worse. I want to know how you saved yourself."

His friend shook his head. "First off, I didn't save myself. Meeting the person who saved me is a story for another day. What I want you to hear today is the final lesson of being a Win Some person."

"If you really think I'm ready, let's do it," Sam agreed. "Wait, I bet we're going back to baseball examples, aren't we?"

Mike gave him a shoulder nudge. "You catch on fast. We're going to do what every ball player does the day after the game."

"Get up slow and creaky, hoping there's still some pain gel left in the medicine cabinet?"

The older man looked startled, then burst out laughing. "No, the other thing you do."

Sam grinned. "I guess you're talking about watching the videos to see how I messed up."

"And you do that to see where you can improve your game. You tell me, is there ever a day after the game when you decide you don't see something to improve?"

Sam snorted, "You're kidding, right? There's always something like turning my hips a second or two sooner or misreading the pitcher. Or there's something I did right and want to see how I can repeat it. No, there's never a day I can't find something to improve."

Mike made a *ta-da* motion with one hand.

"Oh, that's the lesson." Sam nodded his head. "What do you call this step?"

> "Being Win Some isn't something you do once. It is a framework for building fulfilling, satisfying relationships, so everybody can win."

"Step five is the Batting Cage. After every game, you return to the batting cage to reflect on your performance. Once you see the evidence, you can evaluate what worked, diagnose where you need to change, and then adjust your practice to improve. It doesn't matter if every move you made in the game was a success or a miserable failure. You can learn from both outcomes how to achieve success in your next game. As an athlete, you constantly aim for improvement. It's the same with being Win Some."

The sun was a low ball directly in front of them now. Sam plopped his team hat on his head and pulled the brim down to protect his eyes. "So, the Batting Cage reminds me to reflect, assess, and improve each step of the process. Sounds like being Win Some is not a one-and-done."

Mike nodded. "That's right. Being Win Some isn't something you do once. Remember I told you it is a framework for building fulfilling, satisfying relationships, so everybody can win. Going to the Batting Cage gives you the opportunity to think about each encounter to see if you want to make any improvements to create more trust."

> "Every Win Some transaction betters a life."

Sam scratched his chin while he thought about that. "That's why you said we never arrive at our goal because once we assess this new relationship, we'll see how we can improve it."

Mike stood and put one foot on the bench. "Not just new relationships. Old or new, we get satisfaction when we're coming alongside someone to help them. Some days the good will weigh heavier on our side, some days on the other person's scale. But every Win Some transaction betters a life."

"Man, I thought you were kidding when you first talked about being Win Some. But I've seen the changes it's already made in my life. You've convinced me." Sam glanced briefly at a pelican flying low over the waves, then rose to his feet. "And now, we'd better go. I've got to get in the batting cage for real."

Mike laughed, then rounded the table as they headed for their cars. "You've got all the Win Some steps now. I'm proud of you. We can talk again any time you want. And if you have questions, you've got my number."

Alone in his car a few minutes later, Sam reflected on what he'd heard. Mike said he hadn't saved himself. Maybe not, but he had certainly saved Sam's relationships and his job. And Sam was suddenly sure that his friend's lessons would continue shaping his life in ways he had yet to imagine.

CHAPTER TWENTY-SIX

THE GAME PLAN

Sam sat at the kitchen table with his father and son. The two people he loved were unsure why he'd asked them to set aside time to talk.

"Spring training ends this weekend. So, we need to decide how we're going to shape our next few months. We'll all have to be heading north for the regular season. I'm sorry, Ethan, that you won't be able to finish high school here with your friends. But without your mother, I don't have a backup adult for when I can't be here."

"I beg your pardon! I'm an adult and pretty darn responsible if I do say so myself," Richard huffed.

"Sorry, Dad. Of course you're a responsible adult. But do you want to make your home here in Florida? I thought you were looking forward to getting back to Minnesota."

"Well, of course I want to get back home. Connie Gustafson can't keep my trucks running all by herself forever."

Sam snickered. "Really, Dad? Your office manager could run two companies, bring up her own family, run for president, and win American Idol, all while dancing backwards with her hands tied behind her back."

Ethan laughed. "Yeah, Grandpop, from what I've seen, Miss Connie pretty much rules Masterson's Trucking. She even made you give up smelly cheese sandwiches at work."

"Okay, you don't have to rub it in." Richard slouched over the armrests of his wheelchair. "That woman could take on a grizzly armed with only a toothbrush and make him beg for mercy. But Masterson's would be long gone if she hadn't taken up the slack while I've been down here. I'm gonna owe her bigtime when I get home. And she'll never let me forget it."

"Why don't we find out if there's something Connie needs once we get back up north? You could make that part of your thank-you for her help." Sam wasn't above adding a tiny push to move Richard into thinking like a Win Some business owner.

"Sure. So, getting back to this situation from Ethan's point of view. How can he finish school here if you're playing in the Twin Cities and I'm back in Waconia? I still think I should stay here until he graduates." Richard leaned back and smiled at his grandson.

"Wait, do I get a choice in this?" Ethan raised his hand and stared down his father and grandfather.

Sam swiped a hand across his chin to hide a small smile. He was relieved that Ethan was taking enough interest to make his choices known.

"We all get to say what we need to happen next. After the season, we can sit down and figure out what to do over the winter. But let's do this as a team. We can put all the choices and possibilities on the table and discuss them until we find something that works well for us as a family." Sam hoped they would go along with this approach. "So, Ethan, what do you need to make things work for you? It's April and you've got two more months of school."

"Really? I get an opinion?" Ethan checked his dad's face to be sure he was serious. "Okay, you guys don't have to worry about staying here or hiring a *babysitter*," he rolled his eyes, "because finishing high school here isn't that important to me. And yeah, I do plan to finish, so don't panic. Being in school here just happened because you and Mom bought the house and then you went out to Las Vegas to play. But it's not like I have roots here or in this school."

"What do you mean? I thought you like this school and your friends here."

"No, you see, the kids who grew up here and went to school together from kindergarten on know who they are and where they belong. Baseball kids come in for a season or two, then their parents get traded or decide to move to a new team. And we're off again, trying to fit in somewhere new."

"Ethan, I'm so sorry. I never knew you felt that way." Sam's heart pounded at the idea that he'd failed his son in one more way.

"Well, it wasn't that bad, I guess, while Mom was here. At least we were that much of a family. And it got better when Grandpop came down here."

Richard reached out to lay his hand on Ethan's where it rested on the table.

"Look, Dad, it's not your fault. I know you gotta go where the team plays, and all that stuff. I'm used to that. What I'm trying to tell you is that I'd rather be in Minnesota with you and Grandpop. And when you play your away games, maybe Grandpop and I can travel with you." Ethan inspected a hangnail on his thumb. "I just need to know we're a family and we're together."

Sam put his hand on Ethan's shoulder. "I'm glad you told me. I'd rather have the two of you with me, but I didn't want to force you into any more changes before you were ready."

He turned to Richard. "Okay, what secret needs have you been holding onto, Dad?"

Shaking his head, Richard answered, "What any parent and grandparent wants. I'm with Ethan. I'd rather we stay together than separate again. I'm an old man"—he raised his hand to stop their automatic reply—"and I'll deny I said that if you ever repeat it. But this surgery and the turmoil at Bayou forced me to take a hard look at the time I have left. And there's nothing that would make me happier than to spend those days with the two of you. No matter how we work that out or where we end up living."

"Okay," Sam said.

"Wait, I do have one more need. It would break my heart to see Masterson's Trucking go down the drain and all those good people who work for me out of a job. I don't know how much I can manage going forward, but I'd like you to think about helping me out with that, Sam." Richard looked directly at the son who'd chosen baseball over working with his father.

"I promise I'll give that careful thought. And we have time to talk and plan before the end of the season. Will that work for you?" Sam was ready to let go of his regret for not following in his father's footsteps. There was still time for the future to unfold in interesting ways. If he kept assessing where they were and regripping to keep the conversations Win Some, he was sure they could find a compromise. After all, there was a high probability this could be Sam's last season of playing professional baseball.

"Hey, why don't we live with Grandpop in Waconia?" Ethan grabbed his phone off the table and began checking the map. "Did you know it's only an hour from there to the stadium? It's even closer to the airport for when you have away games, Dad."

"Whoa, I'm not sure Grandpop wants us invading his space."

"Oh, I didn't think of that. I just like that town; the lake is cool, and Grandpop said he'd teach me to fish. Do you think we could talk about it?"

Sam looked at his father. "How would you feel about that? We could buy a house. I don't think you'd want us underfoot in your place."

"When can the moving trucks get here?" Richard's grin was huge. "I like how the two of you are thinking. There's a good school system in Waconia. It's close to the cities, and, to tell you the truth, I'd be thrilled to have you back home, Sam. Think you remember how to drive in the snow?"

"Oh man, Minnesota blizzards! You might have to remind me about snow tires after all these years." Sam shook his head and chuckled. "Ethan, if we decide to buy a new place up north, what do you suggest we do with this house? It's your home too." Sam wondered how Ethan would face leaving the last place where his mother had lived with them.

Ethan glanced away, lost in his thoughts. Then he looked at Sam in surprise. "You know what? I don't think I'd mind if we didn't live in this house if that meant we could be closer to Grandpop all the time." Ethan's enthusiasm waned when he stopped to wonder how his father would feel about selling their home. "I mean, if you want to keep this house and spend time here sometimes, that's okay with me too."

"This must be a family choice, Ethan, not just something I want. We're going to set our sights on what our futures look like. You'll be leaving for college sooner than your Grandpop or I would like. But that's your path as you see it now. And Dad, I know you're aching to get back home. So, we're going to do everything possible to help you reach your physical therapy goals and get back to doing what you love."

Ethan realized his dad was working toward an answer, so he thought he would press him. "Dad, what do you need to make these plans work for you?"

Sam looked at the older man and the young man across the table from him. "I'm already getting what I need. I needed a purpose, and the two of you have given me the cornerstone of that. You two and the strength of our family is my top priority. Later, I hope we can build a second pillar that expands that purpose outside the family. But most importantly, I want your trust and love because that allows me to serve you the way you deserve. If moving to Minnesota is the best thing for our family, then I'm all in."

> "Most importantly, I want your trust and love because that allows me to serve you the way you deserve."

"Wow," Ethan said. "That's really deep, but pretty awesome at the same time."

"Thank you." Sam stood and took a bow. Taking his seat again, he asked, "So do we have our Masterson master plan for moving forward?"

He placed his hand palm-down in the center of the table, Ethan slapped his hand on top, and then Richard's gnarled hand topped the stack. "We have a plan." They flipped their hands in celebration.

"Let's each put 'Family Conference' on our weekly schedule. We can sit down and talk things out like we did today, so we don't get off-track with each other again."

"Next time can we have sushi while we talk things over?" Ethan got up and headed to the kitchen.

"Sure. Why don't you call in a takeout order now. I'm hungry." Sam stood and stretched before helping his father roll away from the table into the family room.

"I can work with that. Your request for sustenance has given me purpose."

"So glad I could serve." Sam ruffled the boy's hair on his way past.

Sam hadn't dipped into explaining the Win Some process to them. He hoped they could see his example, so he could gently bring them step-by-step into living their own Win Some lives.

CHAPTER TWENTY-SEVEN

HOPEFUL FUTURE

Sam looked across his backyard, watching his teammates and their families play volleyball and laugh with each other. The kids played Frisbee, tossed bean bags at cornholes, and soaked each other with water balloons. Everyone was blowing off steam, celebrating a strong spring training record before packing up to head north for the regular season.

The massive grill he rented was fired up and ready to roast hot dogs, hamburgers, and veggie kebabs. Lining the back deck were tables of beverages, chips, and all the side dishes and desserts anyone could desire. To top it off, the day was pleasantly warm with a gentle breeze off the water. It was perfect.

One of the catering staff escorted Darla, a huge man, and a small boy through the wide-open back wall of windows and gestured toward Sam.

"Is that your grocery store friend, Sam?" Richard called his attention to the family as they approached. "Well, I got the big bruiser description right. I guess we're about to find out if he's the jealous sort."

"Funny, Dad." Sam stepped forward to greet Darla with a hug. "Glad you could make it, Darla." He turned to her husband. "You must be Tom. It's good to meet you." Then he stooped to shake hands with Benny. "Welcome to my home, Benny. I hope you came ready to have fun today."

Darla beamed with delight and her menfolk looked awed when they realized they were surrounded by most of the Minnesota Millers team.

Sam caught Ethan's attention as he ran past. The boy joined them, panting from exertion and flushed with the sun. "Ethan, I want you to meet my friend Darla, her husband Tom, and their son, Benny."

"Hi! Pleased to meet you. Hey, Benny, you any good at cornhole? I need a partner for the next round."

Benny looked to his mother and father, seeking permission. Tom clapped his hand on the young boy's shoulder and informed them, "Benny is a wiz at cornhole. You couldn't ask for a better partner." He nodded at his son. "Go show 'em how it's done."

Sam introduced Darla and Tom to his father, then said, "Let's get you both something to drink, and then I want you to meet my teammates."

Once he was sure they were comfortably chatting with a group of his friends, he wandered back to the house to make sure everything was ready to go on the grill. When he entered the kitchen, dodging the half-dozen catering crew he'd hired to help, the chef was walking into the room from the direction of the front door.

"Ah, there you are, Mr. Masterson. There's a gentleman here to see you. Says he doesn't want to disturb your party but needs five minutes of your time."

"Did you get his name?" Sam stopped at the sink to wash his hands.

"He said he's Boss Man, if that makes sense." She frowned, unsure she got the message right.

"I know him. You did fine, Cindy. Why don't you and the crew go ahead and get the meat started? We can eat in about half an hour. Once everyone is served, please have your staff sit down and eat with us. I'll be back in a few minutes to help you."

"Sure thing, Mr. Masterson." The caterer started giving orders to her team.

Sam stopped short of the doorway to run his hands through his windblown hair and take a deep breath. Why would Hugh Sutton be at his house the day after the final training game? Of course, he'd invited all the support staff and even sent a printed invitation to his boss's office. But he never expected the man to show up. When he couldn't think of any reason to put off greeting his boss, Sam walked through the family room to the front of the house.

Sutton stood in the foyer, swinging a set of keys on his index finger, dressed for golf.

"Ah, Masterson. There you are." He flashed an unnaturally white smile. "Don't worry, I'm not staying. I think the team and your friends will be more comfortable without the Boss Man watching them party."

"Not at all, sir. We're almost ready to eat." Sam still couldn't get a handle on why the man had shown up at his house.

"Look, I'll make this quick."

Uh-oh, that doesn't sound like good news.

Sutton put his keys in his pockets and rocked back on his heels. "I know we didn't get off to a good start." He looked at Sam to see if he would contradict him.

Sam decided there was nothing he could add to that statement, so he waited for Sutton to continue.

"Well, I can tell you I was surprised by the way you turned things around. And I'm impressed with the way you've mentored Anker. He's shown tremendous improvement, as have some of our other young batters. I hear that's due to you."

"I'm glad you're happy with the young guys. They've worked hard."

"And I've watched you at bat and in the outfield during practices and games. It looks like you've been doing a lot of physical therapy because I can see you're moving that shoulder a lot easier."

"Our team PTs are great, sir. They really helped me recover my range of motion." Sam was worried that his improved shoulder wasn't the point.

"Well, I just wanted to say I'm aware that you've kept your nose clean since that video and done everything the managers and coaches have asked of you. It's like you're a different person. I'm looking forward to seeing what you bring to the season."

Sam was astonished. He'd been sure when Sutton showed up that he was going to be shoving Sam off the team for one reason or another. His shoulders dropped in relief.

"Thank you, sir. I'm eager to get started."

The team owner removed his hat, ran his fingers through his thinning hair, and replaced it. "Well, I'm going to get out of the way so you can get back to your guests."

"You sure you won't stay?"

"Got a date with my golfing buddies. I intend to soak up this sunshine for as long as I can before heading north." He was almost through the door before he turned to say, "We'll talk again at the end of the season, Masterson. I've got something in mind, but it'll wait." Then he trotted over to his low-slung sports car, slipped in, and roared down the driveway.

Well, if that's not a tease, I don't know what is, Sam thought.

Just as his boss walked out the door, Mike came in.

"Sutton came to your party?" Mike looked incredulous.

"Yeah, he stopped by for a moment. We actually had a pleasant conversation. Mike, I can't thank you enough for teaching me to be Win Some. I wouldn't have my job if it weren't for you. Can you imagine if the old me had thrown a party? No one would have shown up." Sam grinned and slung his arm over Mike's shoulder.

When they reached the backyard, Mike wandered toward the grill, shaking hands with Ethan and Richard, then joking with Sam's teammates as he went around the yard.

Sam smiled as he watched his crowd of teammates, family, and friends enjoy the day. Even Darla and Tom were having fun. He'd felt alone for so long. Now he was surrounded by people who cared about him. His eyes landed on Mike, who gave him a thumbs up and mouthed "Go Win Some" before turning back to his conversation with Richard and Jake.

Sam realized that all his efforts to improve his relationships had worked. Today felt like a miracle. However, he suspected there was more to learn about being Win Some and living to serve other people. He couldn't wait to see what happened next.

WIN SOME RELATIONSHIP TOOLS

While Sam, Mike, and the rest of the characters in this book are fictional, Win Some is not. It's a powerful framework for enriching your life, beginning with improving your relationships. Use these steps, and you'll begin to see improvements in all your relationships—even those that have been challenging in the past.

Being Win Some is a continual process of building trust, serving others, and forming healthy relationships. You'll cycle through the steps organically. The more attention you put into being Win Some, the more positive and satisfying your life will become.

THE FIVE TOOL FRAMEWORK FOR FULFILLING RELATIONSHIPS

4 **Runs Batted In**
In Life: **SACRIFICE AND COMMITMENT**
Strive to advance the situation in front of you, helping others and the team reach their goals. Be willing to sacrifice selfish ambitions because commitment to the team is stronger.

3 **At Bat**
In Life: **ASSESS AND RESPOND**
Assess the situation and choose the best emotional tone for that interaction. Re-grip when needed to respond to any anger, distrust, or changing conditions, so you can have a favorable outcome.

2 **On-Deck Circle**
In Life: **CONTROL THE CONTROLLABLES**
Manage your thoughts and emotions to keep them in the present moment. Instead of feeling guilty about the past (which will affect the future), prepare by focusing on your role in the moment, so you can serve.

5

Batting Cage
In Life: **REFLECTIVE GROWTH**
Honestly reflect on your words, deeds, and actions, so you can improve your relationships and outcomes with others. Each time you return to Step 1 and work the *Win Some* tools, your tool set will be stronger and more fulfilling.

1

Grab Your Bat
In Life: **WIN/WIN**
Aim to create win-win situations where you set aside your personal agenda to come alongside others and help them reach their goals, which leads to winning as a team.

The Win Some End Result:
AN EVER-GROWING NUMBER OF ENGAGING AND MEANINGFUL RELATIONSHIPS

ABOUT THE AUTHOR

Brian Slipka is the owner of the True North family of companies, which includes over twenty companies with combined annual revenues of nearly a quarter billion dollars. Slipka graduated from the University of Minnesota's Carlson School of Management, and his early career included sales and leadership positions at major publicly traded companies.

Trusting in the Win Some mindset, he left the public/corporate world and focused on his growing portfolio of small businesses. As the CEO and Managing Partner, Slipka leads a group of diverse main street organizations, as well as their philanthropic arm, True North Family Foundation. He also serves on the boards of several for-profit and non-profit organizations.

Slipka credits his faith, commitment to servant leadership, and ability to build trusting relationships as the bedrock of his success. He resides in Minnesota with his wife, Megan, and their two children.

HORSAGER LEADERSHIP PRESS

Horsager Leadership Press is part of the Horsager Leadership Inc. family of companies, including Trust Edge Leadership Institute.

Based in Saint Paul, Minnesota, our mission is to develop trusted leaders and organizations around the world. Since 1999, we have pioneered leadership development through research, publishing, speaking, human capital development, and consulting, all based on the importance of trust and its proven impact around the world.

Our books aim to inspire and equip leaders and organizations with a high level of trustworthiness.

For research, resources, and tools, call 651-340-6555 or visit HorsagerLeadership.com.